"A house divided against itself cannot stand."

Trumpism and Canada

When did it really emerge, and will it impact our future?

"The overwhelming amount of violent crime in our cities is committed by blacks and Hispanics."

— Donald J. Trump

"We also have no history of colonialism"

— -Stephen J. Harper

Dr. A.Q. Rana, MD, FRCPC, FRCP (HON)

Toronto, Canada

To,

Brian Mulroney, Former Prime Minister of Canada, for his noble work against South African apartheid. Brian Mulroney stood up bravely against apartheid, unlike Conservatives today, who unfortunately support apartheid.

Table of Contents

Preface

Unity is the cornerstone of any strong nation. While countries can overcome challenges such as poverty, famine, and crime through collective effort, a lack of unity can unravel even the most resilient societies. Political polarization is often the precursor to such disunity. When polarization becomes toxic, it not only divides society but also fosters political tribalism — a dangerous phenomenon in which factions form, trust erodes, and democratic institutions face unprecedented challenges.

Contrary to popular belief, a crisis of unity does not just affect minorities. It seeps into the broader fabric of society, disrupting social harmony, economic growth, and progress for all. The repercussions of such divisions are felt by every individual, regardless of their demographic majority or minority status.

Canada, with its unique political landscape shaped by history and a federal parliamentary system, is no stranger to challenges of unity. Provincial disputes and growing distrust between provinces and the federal government in Ottawa have periodically tested the country's cohesion. Additionally, Canada's proximity and close relationship with the United States often mean that major events south of the border have ripple effects here.

The United States, the world's oldest continuous democracy, has endured its share of internal strife, most notably the Civil War. However, political polarization in the US has become increasingly apparent in recent years, especially with the presidency of Donald Trump. The attack on Capitol Hill on January 6th, 2021, was a stark example of how deep divisions can erode democratic norms. Alarmingly, reports suggested that even some Canadians participated in this event, illustrating the influence of US polarization on its northern neighbour.

Many observers argue that Donald Trump's rhetoric and campaigns have been profoundly divisive, exacerbating existing tensions in American society. Polarization along racial, geographic, and socio-economic lines became so pronounced that even politically disengaged individuals could not ignore it. The term "Trumpism" emerged and became synonymous with a particularly corrosive form of political polarization. Worryingly, this ideology found resonance not only in the US but also in other nations, including Canada, New Zealand, and India, where perpetrators of violence against minorities professed admiration for Trump's divisive style of leadership.

While it may seem that Canada's political polarization began with the Trump presidency, and especially from Trump's rhetoric of Canada becoming the 51st state, Trump's attack on Venezuela and kidnapping its president with his wife, and threats to annex Greenland, a closer examination reveals that it has deeper roots. Canadian history is punctuated by political disagreements, conflicts and legislative controversies that have driven divisions long before Trump entered the global stage. However, the last two decades have seen a marked intensification of polarization, beginning with the Harper Conservative era in 2006 and fueled by contentious policies and political debates.

This book examines the trajectory of political division in Canada, from historical disputes to the more recent impact of US polarization on Canadian society. It sheds light on the risks of unchecked polarization in Canada's diverse society and explores how it can threaten the country's unity. A particular focus is placed on the policies and dynamics of Liberal and Conservative governments over the past two decades, along with provincial politics where relevant.

It is important to note that this work is not intended to target or defame any individual, political party, leader, or government. Instead, it aims to provide an objective examination of historical and contemporary political conflicts, many of which have left a lasting impact on Canadian society. The issues discussed in this book are based on publicly available information extensively covered in the news media and academic research. Citations are provided at the end of the book for transparency and accountability.

While the names of individuals have been avoided where possible, they are mentioned when necessary to provide context. This book does not offer definitive conclusions or predictions about the impact of Donald Trump's second presidency or the future trajectory of Canada's political landscape. Instead, readers are encouraged to form their own opinions based on the information and perspectives presented here.

I would like to express my gratitude to everyone who supported me in completing this work. My special thanks go to Renan Levine and Syed S. Islam, professors of political science, and Mr. Syed Imam, attorney at law, for their valuable insights. I am also grateful to Rukaya Ghani, a PhD scholar in political science, Ashley Pearson, Amna Soomro, Zainab Rana, Ahmed Rana and Aamina Masood for providing thoughtful feedback during the drafting process. Finally, I extend my appreciation to my friends Shabbir Razakazee and Mr. Shakir Mohammad, whose unwavering encouragement kept me motivated to finish this book.

Reader's suggestions to improve future editions of this work are welcome, and I hope this book serves as a starting point for meaningful discourse on unity, sovereignty, and the future of Canada.

A.Q. Rana, MD, FRCPC, FRCP (HON)

Toronto, Canada

CHAPTER 1
A Substrate for Political Polarization

Political division can lead to differences in political attitudes arising from extreme political ideologies in any democratic state. Although a norm in any democratic society, political division may become a substrate for further divergence, conflicts, and polarization under different circumstances. To cause polarization, a disagreement should be more than just conflictual, and it must increase the divide between distinct social-partisan groups. In civilized societies, political polarization should be benign, natural, and democratizing under normal circumstances, but sometimes it can become pernicious, causing harm and social unrest.

Polarization augmentation may further conflict, as it creates a divide among groups that are constantly in competition with one another. Polarization is not so much about having different opinions as about refusing to cooperate with another group that holds different ones. Polarization fosters a mentality that divides individuals into groups that indirectly compete against one another. Rather than proceeding to negotiate, extreme polarization may force tribalism onto any society.

An individual's view of political issues depends on their partisanship. This political identity may affect other spheres of their lives that are unrelated to politics. The increase in political partisanship leads to a greater divide within society. This political partisanship, when at extremes, may be expressed through negative emotions and may lead to political violence. Rather than being loyal to their party and respecting the opinions of those around them, this negative partisanship leads individuals to express their anger and engage in outbursts toward the opposing party.

From the viewpoint of political scientists, there are two types of political polarization: elite polarization and mass polarization. Elite polarization is the polarization between the party organizers and elected officials of the party in power and the party in opposition. More often, elite polarization means that there are no ideological similarities among party leaders, and they differ widely on major issues along ideological lines. In contrast, mass polarization affects the electorate, or the general public, and is a popular polarization in which people are divided on political issues and policies along party lines. With mass polarization at its extreme, each group views its opposing party as a threat to society and feels the need to intervene to stop it from endangering the systems.

Some political science experts consider political polarization a top-down process in which elite polarization may lead to mass polarization. However, elite polarization does not necessarily cause popular polarization within the electorate. In a parliamentary system, the polarized political parties are very cohesive and unified as well as ideologically distinct. In a polarized parliament, there is almost no ideological overlap between members of the two parties. The split over legislation and policies runs along a broad ideological divide, leading to the collapse of the ideological center.

Factors Enhancing Political Polarization

Scholars of political science consider many factors that contribute to political polarization in a democratic society, including political parties, mass media, and the political ideology of the people.

Polarization results when political parties adopt positions which are more ideologically distinct, and this can cause polarization among elites as well as among the public. Some political scientists believe that diverging parties have been a major factor in polarization. This becomes especially true when the majority party prioritizes only those positions that are most aligned with its ideology and platform. Currently, such a trend is evident in India. Supporting polarized positions helps politicians because those who align with the more extreme groups within their party tend to stay in office longer. These political leaders further promote polarization to help strengthen their support in a divided society. The polarization is fueled by politicians who promote their views on religion, ethnicity, culture, and many other social issues in diverse societies. These different views, left-wing or right-wing, when broadcast to the public, further promote the divide. Voters who hear these views from politicians feel the need to become emotionally involved in supporting the party, wanting only these politicians to be the leaders. This may lead to the overgrowth of politically defined groups with the intensification of their political ideology. Left- and right-wing voters associate themselves with their groups and possess the mindset that the opposite wing is a threat to society. Their beliefs further divide society, increasing political polarization, as they prefer to associate with those who share similar political beliefs rather than mix with people of different ideologies. Additionally, voters are more polarized by negative statements from leaders of the opposing party than by those from their own party. Like a vicious cycle, this leads political leaders to take more extreme positions.

Some political science scholars believe that in a multiparty system, the extremes of public ideological movements cause further division and lead to highly polarized multiparty systems. This phenomenon of polarized pluralism may lead to further polarization in many opposing directions over policy issues. However, polarization in multiparty systems can also be defined as a division between two ideological extremes, resulting in polarized coalitions of multiple parties on the right or left of the political spectrum.

In a democratic system, people vote for the political leaders who represent their ideology, which is a natural phenomenon. In addition to political ideology, religious, ethnic, and other cultural factors can contribute to the enhancement of polarization. In the United States, for example, the republican voter is more likely to vote for an evangelical candidate, leading to a rise in polarization.

Although political science students disagree, some consider economic inequality a factor influencing public polarization. For example, the Canadian oil industry and the rising issue of climate change have concerned some individuals, while leaving others supporting it. It has caused division in public opinion due to differing views people have towards this subject. For example, the oil industry's role in Alberta's local economy has resulted in significant economic inequalities, contributing to ideological divides. Workers in the energy industry are affected by unfortunate situations in the sector, which align with right-wing parties.

In the United States, the race, as well as the urban and rural divide, has translated into the less affluent rural whites becoming increasingly Republican, while minorities and affluent suburban communities support Democrats. Income may not be the only predictor of the voting preferences in industrial democracies. In the United States, race may predict both the votes and income. Thus, income, in addition to race, may be a good predictor of voting for some racial groups, not income alone.

The growth of mass media has particularly affected the public's voting preferences in recent years and played an influential role in political polarization. In the last few decades, polarization has grown immensely due to the partisan views promoted by the media. The current environment of the mass media has led the audience to move toward more lateralized articles. These broadcasts especially appeal to partisan viewers who like the polarized programming for the gratification of their ideologies. Most social media platforms use search-history-based procedures that polarize certain sources of information for the public. This provides political parties with an advantage in promoting their ideologies to media users and gaining support for partisan views. These changes contribute to increased polarization. In the last couple of decades, fewer partisan viewers are exposed to more polarized news; therefore, countries such as China, with emerging media markets, are becoming more polarized due to the diversification of political media.

Some researchers believe that online media does not increase polarization of opinions. Providing people with impartial information may reduce political polarization, but this effect depends on context. The tone of partisan news sources may affect how different people interpret the same information.

Does Political Polarization Serve a Purpose?

In any democratic society, political polarization can exist as a state or as a process that can accelerate or slow down under different circumstances. When it exists as a state, there is no purpose, and one can assess positive and negative effects. As a process, it has social effects or consequences of decisions made by politicians. The social impacts of political polarization are a subject of debate among students of political science.

Although political polarization is characterized by divisions among individuals within a country, it may also benefit society in various ways. First, political polarization helps scrutinize all policies and can benefit society by subjecting everything to critical review, thereby enhancing accountability. Second, political polarization contributes to addressing injustice and inequalities. Third, political polarization increases voters' enthusiasm for their party leader, and this emotional support benefits politicians. Finally, political polarization, which increases citizens' involvement in the voting process and engagement, is a necessary element of any democratic society. More people engage in their political views and participate in the government, which strengthens the democratic system. Although political polarization can also help overcome internal differences and unite people around a common cause, it risks becoming pernicious, with malignant consequences for society.

Intensification of Political Polarization and Pernicious Polarization

For progress to occur in a society, people need to work on developing and maintaining social institutions that encompass the whole society. This progress in society could be halted due to the aberrant intensification of political polarization. Left-wing voters move further left on the political spectrum, while right-wing voters move further right. This type of hyper-partisanship may negatively affect a society. It may result in a lack of progress and hinder any necessary compromise in the legislative process. Both sides become emotionally involved in the political climate, furthering the divide between the two groups and deepening polarization.

For a diverse society to function smoothly, there needs to be a common approach by the government to all communities and social institutions. The intensification of political polarization may compromise this approach, making it difficult to find common ground. Leaders of opposing parties feed on the support of hyper-partisan individuals to pursue their partisanship, furthering the divide in society and widening the political spectrum. As this divide deepens, many left-wing and right-wing voters prefer to surround themselves with others who share their political views. All aspects of a person's life are now influenced by political polarization. For example, their jobs and the communities they live in are surrounded by similar social circles.

As society is further split by political and personal ideological differences, strong left-wing and right-wing voters become more prominent. These members of society are less likely to compromise their political views and demand that the government's policies align with their ideologies. This only exacerbates polarization, which can significantly weaken the democratic system.

Recently, polarization has been identified as increasing across several democracies, particularly in countries like Brazil, India, Poland, and Italy. These countries have adopted right-wing populist ideologies when making policy changes. What seemed to be center right is now openly turning toward the extreme right. Political leaders such as Narendra Modi in India, and their parties, have tried to undermine opposing parties and further only their own interests. The polarization adopted in these countries is further pushing apart the opposing wings, turning their ideologies into extremism, harming the citizens of the country, and slowly damaging their democratic system.

Political polarization has also been on the rise in the United States and has particularly become malignant since Donald Trump became President. Polarization has grown immensely over the decades and has now raised concerns about its democratic future. In 1992, communities in the United States had a near-symmetrical balance between right- and left-wing supporters. As people became increasingly interested in government and polarization grew, the 2020 and 2024 presidential elections further intensified the country's tribalism. As the US shifted towards a more polarized ideology, individuals in the country tend to surround themselves with people who are more likely to agree with them on various subjects, including views on the world and politics. It is this framework of polarization; one closes oneself off from others and diminishes the potential for dialogue with others who represent difference.

Since polarization as a process can increase or decrease under different circumstances, it can become pernicious. When polarization turns pernicious, most political scholars believe it is due to a single factor which outweighs other divides in a pluralistic political life. Sometimes, the factors causing pernicious polarization may not be ideological, such as globalist versus patriotic and nationalist, or urban versus rural. These political divides lead to mutual distrust between the two political parties and, beyond the political domain, affect people's social relations.

Polarization may also become pernicious during the processes of removing a leader by political elites. Since pernicious polarization is characterized by much deeper societal penetration, it reinforces itself over time, becoming a vicious cycle that pulls society further into division.

Pernicious polarization makes it difficult for political elites on both sides of the divide to find common ground. It weakens people's trust in the democratic system and may halt the legislative process. Pernicious polarization may undermine the judicial system's nonpartisan position. It leads to a lack of trust in the political parties, intolerance, discrimination, increased risk of violence, and social unrest. In democracies where political accountability is weak and politics is self-referential, the winner uses all means to exclude the losing party as a future risk. Since people start aligning themselves only with the messages of their own bloc, facts and moral truth become controversial. In such an atmosphere, academics and journalists also take partisan positions, which erodes public confidence in these institutions. People find it difficult to act in a morally truthful fashion if it conflicts with their party's interests. In these circumstances, political polarization becomes less amenable to resolution.

The intensification of political polarization, driven by politicians, undermines democratic institutions. Members of the justice system may develop biases rather than remain neutral. The decisions made by politicians, driven by hyper-partisan interests, benefit their party rather than the whole country. This type of political atmosphere breeds distrust between the two parties, who view each other as threats to society.

The intensification of political polarization increases political rivalry and may contribute to a spike in hate crimes and violence between the right-wing and left-wing, disturbing the peace of society. It can lead to accepting public discrimination, destroying social trust, violence to partake in society, and allowing truth to lose its value when people choose to follow only their group's particular message.

Members of society divide along party lines, leading to many conflicts and a negative view of various issues. Intensification of political polarization has led to toxic disagreements in society, pitting citizens against one another and destroying the country's social climate.

As polarization increases, it threatens the democratic system, as has recently been seen in the United States. This was obvious in the 2020 US presidential elections and on January 6th, 2021, when the Capitol Hill in Washington, DC was attacked. As members of society become more aware of the political climate and engage in politics, they are increasingly believing that democratic institutions lack political diversity, leading to a loss of trust in the democratic system.

The country's ability to solve problems becomes increasingly complex as polarization escalates, affecting decision-making. Because political opinions are so sharply divided, it becomes difficult for individuals to agree on solutions for the greater good of society. Rather than thinking of what is beneficial to the country, they tend to focus on what is better for their political career and their party. Like a vicious cycle, the problem of failing to find solutions to issues continues to widen polarization in society.

CHAPTER 2

Origin of Conflicts

Although many believe that political polarization has grown exponentially in Canada since Donald Trump became president of the US in 2017, politically influenced violence has a long history in Canada, even before the Confederation of Canada. For instance, there were rebellions in Quebec and Ontario in 1837 and 1838. Although the list may be long, only some of the conflicts have been mentioned in this section.

European Contact and Beginning of Conflicts

Before European colonization, Indigenous peoples inhabited the land and had developed their own cultures, governments, traditions, and languages. They lived in coherence for thousands of years on their own land. The three main divisions of Indigenous peoples were the Inuit, Métis, and First Nations, divided among the regions where they lived. These communities had their own spiritual beliefs and organizations within their societies. They used the natural world to supply their resources and meet their social needs.

Indigenous lifestyles began to change as European explorers made their way across the Atlantic and settled in Indigenous peoples' homelands. Although there were a few earlier European settlements temporarily located in Canada for fishing, permanent settlements from European colonies began in the late fifteenth century. Over centuries, different Europeans invaded the Indigenous land and stripped them of their culture and lifestyle as they colonized Canada. Elements of the different cultures and other migrant groups combined to form what is now known as the mosaic Canadian culture.

Originally, the first Europeans, the Norse Vikings, arrived in North America in the 11th century, sailing from Iceland and Greenland and settling on the coast of Newfoundland and Labrador. The purpose of the settlement was temporary: to hunt and fish. As Indigenous people became aware of one another's settlements, they managed to live in peace, maintaining a trade agreement. Their settlement did not last long; they left two years later due to conflict with Indigenous people. The Indigenous people had a bigger advantage in the Canadian land and were able to drive the settlers out of their settlements due to their disagreement. The European settlers were not prepared to fight against the Indigenous peoples as they had less experience on Canadian land and did not have the right resources to fight.

As centuries passed, English, French, and Portuguese explorers continued to explore Canada's Atlantic coast. Italian navigator John Cabot landed in Newfoundland in 1497 and took possession of the land for England. Although the Portuguese Empire claimed Newfoundland and Labrador, they shifted their focus to South America, leaving North America behind. In 1534, Jacques Cartier proceeded to explore the Gulf of St. Lawrence on behalf of the King of France. Cartier left for France and returned the next year to continue his navigation of Canada. He tried to establish a settlement near Quebec City from 1541 to 1543, but was unable to achieve this due to the Iroquoian people.

By the halfway point of the 16th century, European explorers had already occupied land along parts of Newfoundland and Labrador's coasts and the Gulf of St. Lawrence. To support peace with the First Nations, they established trade relations to exchange resources. Settlers from England, France, Holland, and Sweden managed to occupy land across the Atlantic Coast. Due to the emerging economy, François Du Pont-Gravé and Pierre Du Gua De Monts hired the geographer Samuel de Champlain to establish trading posts to support their expeditions. Alliances built between the French and Indigenous peoples helped the French further their establishments. As Champlain allied himself with the Algonquin nation in 1608 to secure a trading post in the St. Lawrence Valley, he was forced to bring forces and participate in the war against the Iroquois. As France made an Alliance with the Algonquin nation, the Iroquois made an Alliance with the Dutch settlers who settled near Iroquois territory.

The arrival of Europeans set the stage for the ongoing conflicts with Indigenous people, and the effects of colonialism continue to be reproduced in contemporary society by different means. This led to continuous oppression, land grabbing, persecution of Indigenous leaders, the murder of women and children, as well as an apartheid which is viewed as the darkest part of our history by many Canadians, including those of European origin, who believe in justice and peace.

Iroquois – French Conflict

As the voyages were underway, Champlain aided the Huron-Wendat and Algonquin in forming alliances with French colonists and merchants. The Fur Trade Economy had begun to create conflict between different First Nations. The Iroquois tribe had the power of Dutch traders to aid them by providing firearms for hunting to participate in the fur trade. Using these new resources, they tried to exert military pressure on the Mohican tribe to expand their territory. Different First Nations groups were now in conflict with one another, raiding one another's land. The Mohawk and Oneida attacked the colonies throughout the St. Lawrence Valley, allied with the Algonquin. To stop the raids, the French began establishing settlements upriver toward Montreal.

Quebec City, Capital of New France

In 1608, Samuel de Champlain founded the capital of New France, now known as Quebec City. He handled the city's affairs and administration and continued to send explorers to further expand their territory.

English Colony of Newfoundland

Newfoundland was claimed to be the first English colony in North America, as Humphrey Gilbert claimed the land in the Queen's name in 1583. France challenged Humphrey Gilbert's claim to Newfoundland, which led to the establishment of several settlements. Throughout the 17th and 18th centuries, various voyagers settled in Newfoundland, some of whom were planned while others were only there for its fishing port. As different voyagers occupied the land, the Treaty of Paris settled the challenge amongst colonies. In 1763, the Treaty of Paris granted Newfoundland to England. As the French had managed to claim various lands in Canada, such as Nova Scotia and Ville-Marie, the 1763 Treaty of Paris declared that all French claims were surrendered to the English.

Conflict of English and French – The Abolition of the Rights of the French-speaking in 1774

In 1763, the Royal Proclamation laid the fundamentals for governing the North American territories that France had surrendered to Britain. In the 1763 Treaty of Paris, the French surrendered their land to Britain after the Seven Years' War. The Royal Proclamation established Quebec as a province and declared that the British would have more power than the French. One of the main objectives of the proclamation was to assimilate the French-speaking Canadians into British society. The proclamation also recognized British power over Canada and Quebec, declaring that Quebec would be governed by the British and that the French would not be allowed to govern unless they proved their loyalty to the British. The British leaders of Canada controlled the French's property and removed the religious, political, and social rights of the French-speaking Canadians.

The Quebec Act of 1774 reversed the Royal Proclamation. The purpose of this Act was to give the French the rights they had lost in the Royal Proclamation: the freedom to worship and the right to property. As the Royal Proclamation failed, Governors James Murray and Lord Guy Carleton decided to use the Quebec Act of 1774 to gain the French's loyalty to the British Parliament. The Quebec Act allowed French Catholics to obtain government jobs, which had been prohibited by the Royal Proclamation. It allowed the French to practice law as they preferred and to exercise control.

American – British Conflict

In 1783, the Treaty of Paris declared that Britain would surrender modern-day Michigan, Illinois, and Ohio to the Americans. While Britain claimed French land, it refused to acknowledge the part of the treaty concerning American land. They located military posts on the Great Lakes surrounding the area they had to surrender to the US. The conflict between the two nations erupted as the

British restricted US trade while providing native allies with ammunition. America's desire to expand its territory into land the British were unwilling to surrender resulted in the War of 1812.

The War of 1812 was fought between the United States and Great Britain on Canadian soil. The United States had many victories, retaking Detroit in 1813 and driving the British out of Western Ontario. The War of 1812 ended as negotiations between the two nations took place. The United States offered to end impressment, and Britain promised to withdraw from the Canadian border and surrender American territory. Canadians and the Native Americans were impacted the most by the conflict between the two nations.

Rebellions Against the British

The rebellions of 1837 and 1838 took place against the government in both Upper and Lower Canada.

In 1837, Louis-Joseph Papineau led patriots, French-Canadian nationalists, to dominate the Legislative Assembly. They continued their rebellion against the British governor and demanded control over the colony's spending. Many of their political demands were rejected, prompting more protests and rallies across the colony. The Rebellion of 1837 resulted in two violent events. In November of 1837, the rebels fought British regulators and were defeated. The second event, set in November of 1838, also ended in their defeat. In both violent acts, the rebels were too disorganized to achieve victory.

William Lyon Mackenzie led the Upper Canadian rebellion in 1837. He and his followers challenged the land grants favoured to Britain's settlers rather than building relations with the US. As years of peaceful protests yielded no action from the government, Mackenzie led them in an attempt to seize power. Mackenzie and 200 followers travelled to the US and accepted American volunteers' help to raid Upper Canada. Eventually, their rebellion was defeated.

United Province of Canada

Lord Durham was sent by the British government to analyze the rebellions of 1837 and 1838 and to provide direction in the Durham Report on further steps to take. By the 1840 Act of Union, Britain united Upper and Lower Canada into the Province of Canada. The two colonies were governed as part of the province and were included in the 1867 Confederation of Canada.

The Great Migration of Canada Increases Tensions Between Indigenous and Immigrants

Between 1815 and 1850, the population of Canada boomed as over 800,000 European immigrants migrated to and settled in Canada. Most immigrants were British settlers, with many from Ireland as well, to escape the Irish Famine. The Great Migration was the result of many factors. The Irish migrated due to the famine that erupted in Ireland. The Industrial Revolution was a major factor in the migration of people to Canada, as lower-class individuals had difficulty finding employment in their countries. The dynamism of the Industrial Revolution created opportunities for immigrants to find jobs in Canada. The wealthy classes benefited from the migration, driven by Canada's natural resources, which provided multiple business opportunities. Therefore, immigrants who settled in Canada during this time were all seeking a better life for their families and themselves. Migration continued to increase tensions between the Indigenous and immigrant communities.

Pacific Colonies

In 1774 and 1775, Spanish explorers travelled along the Pacific Northwest Coast. Bodega y Quadra travelled along the coast of British Columbia and Alaska, preparing maps and charts of the land. By the time the Spanish decided to build a fort on Vancouver Island, British navigator James Cook had mapped the coast as far as Alaska. Although James Cook was not the first to explore the Northwest Coast, he was the first to find its attractions.

CHAPTER 3

John A. Macdonald Era

Political polarization in Canada has greatly fluctuated over time. Political differences, disagreements, disputes, conflicts, and scandals involving various governments at times contributed to the rise of political polarization in Canada. The political polarization in Canada has dramatically increased in the last two decades under both conservative and liberal governments, leading to several incidents of political violence. It has become more intense since Donald Trump's first presidency in 2017.

The Confederation of Canada was created on July 1st, 1867, consisting of three British North American Colonies: Nova Scotia, New Brunswick, and the Province of Canada, forming the Dominion of Canada. The three colonies were then divided into four provinces, with Nova Scotia and New Brunswick becoming their own provinces, and the Province of Canada splitting into Ontario and Quebec. Between 1867 and 1949, the country grew to include ten (10) other provinces and three (3) territories.

The idea of Canada's Confederation was discussed shortly after the American Civil War had ended. The control of the United States of America over British North America instilled fear in the country, as the

American Civil War cast the US government in a weak light. This idea inspired Canada's dominion in hopes of Canada having a strong government for its British North American colonies. As America won the war, Canada feared US expansion into Canadian territories, and much discourse circulated on the topic. Many conferences were held to confirm the Confederation of Canada to occur in 1867.

Incidents of politically influenced violence continued to take place from time to time after the confederation. For example, in the latter part of the 19th century, there were Red River Rebellions and the Northwest Rebellions in Manitoba. In the early decades of the 20th century, there were also many labour conflicts in many cities across the country. Although the list may be extensive, only some of the conflicts are mentioned in the following sections.

Due to a high degree of political legitimacy and the stability of the Canadian democratic system, violent incidents that have persisted for longer periods have been much fewer than in many other countries. The racial conflicts, moral, and financial scandals led to division, hyper-partisanship, polarization, and distrust of the democratic system.

The episodic growth of political polarization in Canada has been due to many factors, such as Indigenous rights, sentiment of separation in Quebec and Alberta, abuse of minorities, and Canada's foreign policy, among other problems. Political polarization leads to a rise in violence towards members of the state or civilians within the country. Although growing political polarization has been a root cause of various issues in Canadian society, it remains less prevalent in Canada than in the United States of America.

John A. Macdonald

John Alexander Macdonald served as the first prime minister from 1867 to 1873 and from 1878 to 1891. He was born in Scotland, and his family immigrated to Kingston, Province of Upper Canada, now known as Ontario. He was a lawyer and was involved in the establishment of the Confederation of Canada on July 1st. 1867. He is known for establishing the North-West Mounted Police, annexing the North-Western Territory, Rupert's Land, British Columbia, and Prince Edward Island. In 1873, he resigned amid allegations that he had accepted a bribe from a businessman to award the contract to build the Canadian Pacific Railway. He was re-elected in 1878. He is known for building a national government. He is criticized for the execution of the Métis leader Louis Riel, which alienated many francophones from his Conservative Party. He is also criticized for his role in the Chinese head tax, the oppression of Indigenous people, his role during the North-West Rebellion, and being the architect of the residential school system, all known as dark chapters in Canadian history.

Public Records

PACIFIC SCANDAL

Between 1872 and 1873, the Pacific Scandal occurred following the Confederation agreement with British Columbia in 1871. The scandal accused Prime Minister John A. Macdonald and members of his conservative government of accepting bribes to influence the construction of the Canadian Pacific Railway. The money was given to Macdonald and other members of the government. Although Macdonald dismissed these claims as false, evidence was found that he accepted the money as a bribe for the railway.

A railway builder and a shipping magnate donated more than $350,000 to the Conservative campaign in the promise that he would be rewarded with the Canadian Pacific Railway contract. He had kept records of all his transactions, including the one he had made with Prime Minister Macdonald, as well as the agreement the two parties had discussed. He was to be rewarded with the contract of building the Canadian Pacific Railway in exchange for the funds provided for the conservative campaign.

Once the scandal broke out in April of 1873, Canadians began to lose trust in the government. As various members of the conservative government were involved in the Pacific Scandal, people did not trust the party as a whole for its involvement in financial corruption. As an investigation was in progress, Prime

Minister Macdonald was fairly certain he was at a major disadvantage with the evidence presented, and he resigned from the Conservative government.

CREATION OF THE RCMP AND SUPPRESSION OF INDIGENOUS PEOPLE

In 1873, the North-West Mounted Police, now known as the Royal Canadian Mounted Police (RCMP), was created by John A. Macdonald. The RCMP is Canada's federal police force, and its purpose was initially to enforce federal law and sovereignty in the West. In its origin, the duties of the NWMP were to maintain order in the North-West provinces and suppress the population of Indigenous peoples. The NWMP was tasked to stop any opposition that posed a threat to the country.

RED RIVER AND NORTHWEST REBELLIONS

In 1869 and 1870, the Red River colony rebelled against the Canadian government, a rebellion triggered by the transfer of Rupert's Land to the new country of Canada from the Hudson's Bay Company. The Métis commenced the Red River Rebellion, led by Louis Riel.

In 1885, the Métis rebelled against the Canadian government by taking part in the Northwest Rebellion. The rebellion was led by Louis Riel, who led a five-month uprising against the Canadian government over the rapid changes they had brought to the West. Louis Riel united all individuals, Metis and non-Métis, to bring their concerns to Prime Minister Macdonald regarding government changes to provinces such as Manitoba, Alberta, and Saskatchewan. Multiple battles took place between the rebels and the NWMP, which resulted in hundreds of casualties. Eventually, the rebellion ended when federal troops defeated them. The suppression of this rebellion strengthened the control of the prairies and demonstrated the authority of the national government. However, it lost the Conservative Party's support in Quebec, leading to distrust of the Anglophone community.

RESERVES AND THE INDIAN ACT – DIVISION, OPPRESSION AND CONFLICTS

The Indian Act was introduced in 1876 to suppress First Nation cultures and assimilate them into the Euro-Canadian society by force. The Indian Act included various human rights violations of the Indigenous peoples, controlling their identities. The act forced First Nation children into residential schools where they would learn to live in Euro-Canadian culture. It made it illegal to hold their religious ceremonies and openly practice their traditions. The act made it agonizingly difficult to claim land, and they could not hire lawyers to help them in this process. The Department of Indian Affairs handled all decisions, including Indigenous peoples' rights. Additionally, it was extremely difficult for them to keep the status of 'Indian,' and if they were to do so, they would lose several other rights. The act violated their rights in hopes that it would demolish their culture, and they would adapt to the Euro-Canadian culture.

As a result of the Indian Act, the Indigenous population grew isolated from the new settlers and Canada's general population. Over the decades, the act was amended multiple times, and in the late 20th century, many rights that had been initially violated were restored to First Nations. This did not reverse all the damage the Indian Act has caused, as it created a divide between First Nations and the rest of the Canadian population that never mended.

RESIDENTIAL SCHOOLS AND INTERGENERATIONAL TRAUMA

The Canadian government established the residential school system under the Indian Act. These schools were run by churches to educate the children of Indigenous peoples to adopt "white man's" culture and assimilate them into Euro-Canadian values. Residential schools were established in the 1830s to force the Indigenous youth to Euro-Canadian customs and potentially convert them to Christianity. This was the government's way of reducing native culture and completely exterminating their traditions within the next few generations. Over 130 residential schools were managed from 1831 to 1996, with approximately 150,000 Indigenous children attending these schools.

Before the actual establishment of the residential schools, Indigenous leaders hoped their children would adapt to Euro-Canadian schooling to learn how to exist in Canadian society. Unfortunately, residential schools were not what Indigenous leaders expected, as their children were physically and sexually abused and stripped of their culture. Upon their leave, the Indigenous youth were separated from their parents for 10-12 months in the year. Once school commenced, they were immediately stripped of practicing their traditions in school; they were forbidden to speak their language, barred from wearing traditional clothes, and children were even stripped of their birth name and forced to adopt an English name.

The Indigenous youth were met with decades of abuse from residential schooling. Students were physically abused, and the punishments were imposed by the wrongful power of the staff. Children were sexually abused by school staff members who faced no consequence when allegations were brought forward. Students were malnourished and vulnerable to diseases such as Influenza or Tuberculosis. These schools were poorly funded; students had to work and were forced to have strict discipline. Students were deprived of their identity and were forced to change their lifestyle to accommodate the Euro-Canadian society. Thousands of children died in these schools, and many of their bodies were not returned to their families. In 2015, the Truth and Reconciliation Commission released a report that found a significant lack of goals and standards in education, and that the curriculum was irrelevant to children's needs. These schools made the Indigenous children feel insecure and disoriented.

The Indigenous youth in the residential schools were isolated from their identities. Forced to leave their parents and traditions behind, the students had to adapt to a whole new lifestyle and took on years of humiliation and abuse. The trauma derived from residential schooling passed through generations, impacting the entire Indigenous population. Survivors of residential schools demanded that the government acknowledge the roles it had played in the prolonged suffering of the youth. Though the government's knowledge of the suffering is acknowledged, it does not replace the torture Indigenous youth had to endure.

CONFLICT OF MANITOBA SCHOOLS

The Manitoba Act of 1870 was enacted to outline the laws governing educational institutions in Manitoba and to protect religious schools. The act stated that such schools would be funded by provincial taxes. Additionally, the Manitoba Act of 1870 declared that English and French would be the province's official languages and would be taught in schools.

As time progressed, the Métis left their home in Manitoba after Manitoba joined the Confederation, migrating west. Their departure led to a larger expansion of the English-speaking settlers' territory. The increase of English-speaking settlers led the French-speaking community of Manitoba to become a minority. In the 1880s-1890s, the government enforced a new immigration policy, led by D'Alton McCarthy, that favoured British supremacy and favoured immigration by the anglophone majority, leaving the French-speaking population in Manitoba to gradually decline. In March of 1890, the official language of Manitoba was changed to solely English.

The change in government affected the Manitoba Act on education, resulting in the Manitoba Schools Crisis. In March of 1890, the government passed two new bills regarding the province's education: the Act Respecting the Department of Education, which eliminated the Board of Education and created the Department of Education, and the Act Respecting Public Schools, which eliminated religious school districts.

This left the Catholic population, mostly French, to fund their own schools to receive education on their religion. Public schools were now the majority, and they did not include religious education. Additionally, schools were not allowed to teach or speak any language other than English. The French struggle in Manitoba's 'school crises' was one of the most significant events in Canadian history. This created great disappointment in Manitoba's French-speaking community, and skepticism between the two communities persisted.

CHAPTER 4

Robert Borden Conservative Era (1911-1920)

Robert Laird Borden was born in Grand-Pré, Nova Scotia and served as the eighth prime minister of Canada from 1911 to 1920. He initially worked as a schoolteacher and later completed his law degree. He was elected to the House of Commons in 1896, representing the Conservative Party. He is known for leading Canada during the First World War.

Public Records

CONSCRIPTION CRISIS OF 1917 – ENGLISH AND FRENCH DIVIDE

The Conscription Crisis is an important conflict in Canadian history which resulted in a divide of public opinion. This issue motivated the people of Quebec to believe that Canada was not a nation of two cultures. Additionally, the Conscription Crisis helped trigger Quebec's independence movement, which became more popular in the 1960s-70s.

With the First World War beginning in 1914, over 330,000 Canadians volunteered to fight on behalf of Canada. Midway through the war, the casualty rate of the soldiers began to increase rapidly, and concern began to escalate as there were not enough volunteers to join soldiers in the frontlines. Prime Minister Robert Borden believed that conscription was needed to get enough soldiers from Canada to perform their full duty in the war.

British-born Canadians enlisted in larger numbers, while Canadian-born Canadians and French Canadians were in fairly small numbers. Prime Minister Borden believed the best way to win this war was to announce a compulsory service. The difficult task was to secure the votes to proceed with conscription, as the Liberals opposed it, knowing that Quebec would not be in favour of this service. Prime Minister Borden proceeded with the law by convincing members of the Liberal Party. Although Quebec opposed conscription, British-born and English-speaking Canadians supported it, allowing Prime Minister Borden to pass the law on August 29th, 1917.

French Canadians were conscripted into fighting during the Great War on their country's behalf. As Canada made a significant contribution to the war, the Quebec population felt isolated from the rest of the country, experiencing a cultural divide between the two. Because the English supported the war and the French did not, conscription passed, disregarding French concerns. The compulsory service led by Prime Minister Borden led to the significant political Conscription Crisis supporting Great Britain in the First World War.

For centuries, the Francophone community has not forgotten the mistreatment it received from the federal government of Canada. The First World War was more than a war among different countries; it was when French Canadians discovered that Canada was not a country of unity between the two communities. The English dominated them, and this was not forgotten when, decades later, Quebec pursued an independence movement to gain full sovereignty for its province.

DETENTION OF MUSLIMS IN INTERNMENT CAMPS IN THE FIRST WORLD WAR

The Muslim community has been reported to have been living in Canada as early as 1851. The Muslim population tended to settle in the community of Lac La Biche, Alberta, and London, Ontario. Like most minority groups in Canada during this time, Muslim immigrants faced a lot of discrimination from the government.

As the First World War began, Muslims were sent to an internment camp in Kapuskasing, Ontario. Though historical records have shown that Muslims fought in the war on behalf of Canada, most of the population was sent to these camps, just as immigrants of other various backgrounds were at the time, to further eliminate any risk or threat to Canada during the war. Canada had established concentration camps for immigrants due to prejudice and paranoia about the minorities.

Immigrants of different backgrounds, including Muslims, were detained in these camps where they were held during the First World War. When a labour shortage erupted as the men who operated the services were sent to war, the detainees were forced out of the camps and into factories in unsafe conditions to continue operations. The various camps operating across Canada continued until 1920.

MUSLIMS PROHIBITED FROM SOCIALIZING WITH INDIGENOUS PEOPLE – DIVIDING THE TWO COMMUNITIES

Muslim immigration to Canada dates to 1851, as Muslim immigrants moved to the West to further establish their businesses and engage in Canada's economy. Muslim immigrants who settled in the West maintained good relations with the Indigenous people by trading along the Mackenzie River and establishing marital relationships with them. These relationships put them in a difficult position with the Hudson Bay Company. The company decided to pressure the Interior Minister to create a law to ban Muslim's trading with the Indigenous peoples to minimize their relations.

The goal of the Hudson Bay Company was to limit the relations between the Muslim community and Indigenous peoples due to their own conflict with the Indigenous community. Rather than letting the trade continue with the two minorities, they demanded control over the Muslim population, who traded and contributed to the economy. The steps taken by the Interior Minister led to a divide between the two groups, which only deepened over time.

WOMEN'S RIGHT TO VOTE – MANITOBA TAKES THE LEAD

January 28th, 1916, marks the day when the first province in Canada allowed women the right to vote. After decades of struggle, Manitoba declared women the right to vote in federal elections. Although First Nations, Inuit, and Asian women were still unable to vote, it was a big step for the Canadian government in the direction of gender equality. Declared in Manitoba's entry to Confederation in 1870 that women would not be able to vote in any election, the women's suffrage movement grew through campaigns and protests against gender inequality. This movement was led by women's rights activists who continuously pursued equality for women. The lead taken by Manitoba set a path for other provinces to follow, giving women the right to vote. Unfortunately, it was a long road before women from different minority groups could vote.

QUEBEC WOMEN'S SUFFRAGE LAGS

Women's suffrage was the movement for women's right to vote. Women continuously protested discrimination and gender inequality in the late 19th century. The first province to grant women the right to vote was Manitoba in 1916, followed by Saskatchewan and Alberta. In succession, every province except Quebec followed Manitoba's steps. Quebec women were unable to vote until 1940, when Bill 18 was passed. Racism has a long history in Quebec and occasionally manifested into sexism and other forms of inequality.

PARIS PEACE CONFERENCE IN 1919

After the First World War, Canadian Prime Minister Robert Borden insisted on sending Canadian delegates to the Paris Peace Conference, along with delegates from other countries. This request was met with opposition from the United States of America and France. British Prime Minister David Lloyd George worked to convince the Americans to allow delegates from other countries, such as Canada, India, New Zealand, and South Africa, to have seats at the conference. Although Canada had little input in the actual peace negotiations amongst all members, it was an active ally and contributor in the First World War. It gained sovereignty from its participation in the war.

CHAPTER 5

William Lyon Mackenzie King / R. B. Bennett Era (1921-1948)

William Lyon Mackenzie King served as the tenth Prime Minister of Canada for three non-consecutive terms from 1921 to 1926, 1926 to 1930, and 1935 to 1948. He was born in Kitchener, Ontario. He obtained a law degree in 1896. He was best known for his leadership in Canada throughout the Great Depression and the Second World War. He played a major role in laying the foundations of the Canadian welfare state and is the longest-serving prime minister, with a total of 21 years and 154 days in office.

He was elected to the House of Commons in 1908 and became the Minister of Labour in 1909 under Prime Minister Wilfrid Laurier. After Laurier's death in 1919, he became leader of the Liberal Party. He unified the party's pro- and anti-conscription groups, leading it to victory in the 1921 federal election. He established a post-war agenda, lowered wartime taxes and tariffs, and strengthened Canadian autonomy. In 1926, facing a House of Commons vote to resign, he asked Governor General Lord Byng to dissolve parliament and call an election. This was refused, and Conservatives were invited to form a government, which soon lost a motion of no confidence. These events created a constitutional crisis, the King–Byng affair. Following this, King and the Liberals won the 1926 election. He made Canada's foreign policy more independent and introduced need-based old-age pensions. King's reaction to the Great Depression led to a defeat in the 1930 election, but the Conservative government grew unpopular, and King had a major victory in the 1935 election. He negotiated the 1935 Reciprocal Trade Agreement with the United States, introduced the National Housing Act, unemployment insurance, family allowances, and the first universal welfare program. His government also established Trans-Canada Air Lines, now known as Air Canada, and the National Film Board. He led Canada during the Second World War and negotiated Newfoundland's entry into Confederation. After leading Canada for more than 21 years, he retired from politics in late 1948.

Public Records

THE GREAT DEPRESSION – SUFFERING OF WESTERN CANADA

The Great Depression severely impacted Canada. Between 1929 and 1933, many businesses were closed due to tremendous financial losses. Canadian imports and exports decreased, construction had dramatically ceased, and wholesale prices had dropped. The Great

Depression resulted in 20% of the population becoming dependent on government assistance.

In 1930, Prime Minister Mackenzie King chose not to provide financial aid to the provinces. This caused widespread distrust of the government, and the Liberal Party lost the election, resulting in a Conservative victory. New Conservative Prime Minister Richard Bedford Bennett decreased federal spending and failed to manage the depression. In the 1935 election, the Liberal Party won the election again, and the Liberal government of Mackenzie King passed the 1935 Reciprocal Trade Agreement with the US. It helped develop economic relations between Canada and the United States of America, reversing the 1930-1931 trade war. The federal government established programs to provide relief, including the National Employment Commission and the National Housing Act. In 1936, the Canadian Broadcasting Corporation became a crown corporation. In 1937, Trans-Canada Airlines, now known as Air Canada, was established. In 1938, parliament transformed the Bank of Canada from a private entity to a crown corporation. Although many new developments took place, Western Canada was still a long way from achieving full economic recovery.

ESTABLISHMENT OF WORKING CAMPS - "ON-TO-OTTAWA TREK" PROTEST

During the Great Depression, the Bennett Government established working camps in which unemployed single men were exploited to construct roads and other public works at low wages. These camps provided the men with daily meals, housing, and medical care in exchange for endless hours of labour. This created suspicion of the government due to its failure to provide appropriate workplace conditions and pay workers appropriate wages. Workers united in 1933, forming the popular protest "On-to-Ottawa Trek" to bring their demands to the parliament. Many individuals from Western Canada joined them. The riots erupted in Regina, Saskatchewan, when a policeman and a protester were executed, along with many others injured.

The riots and trials between the strikers and the government resulted in the loss of Bennett's Conservative Government in the 1935 Federal Election. Shortly after, the working camps were dismantled and replaced with relief camps. Although the Trek could not reach Ottawa, several of their demands were addressed. Owing to their riots, social and welfare provisions emerged through public support.

LEGISLATIVE AUTONOMY OF CANADA - BRITISH AUTHORITY OVER SOME CONSTITUTIONAL CHANGES

In 1931, the British Parliament passed the Statute of Westminster. This statute provided Canada with almost complete autonomy from the United Kingdom. Although the Statute of Westminster was passed in 1931, the United Kingdom still retained some authority over certain constitutional changes in Canada, but this authority was relinquished after the Canada Act of 1982. The Canada Act led the country to full sovereignty.

DETENTION OF JAPANESE IN THE SECOND WORLD WAR – DISCRIMINATION TOWARD MINORITIES

Canada joined World War Two against Germany on September 10th, 1939. Canada provided munitions to help guard the North Atlantic Ocean against the Germans and supplied forces for the invasions of Italy and France in 1943. Over one million Canadians joined the armed forces in World War Two. More than 43,000 died, and another 55,000 were wounded.

After the war began with Japan in December 1941, the Canadian government began the Japanese Canadian Internment. The internment relocated 22,000 Canadian residents of Japanese descent to camps in the British Columbia region. This relocation subjected Japanese Canadians to curfews and interrogations designated by the government, loss of jobs and properties, or deportation back to Japan. Although the Canadian military reported that most of the Japanese population was not a risk to the security of other Canadians, the government continued to send Japanese Canadians to internment camps. This issue served nothing but continuous policies of racism against the minority group, violating their human rights.

NEWFOUNDLAND JOINED CANADA

The Great Depression led the Dominion of Newfoundland to surrender its self-governing status in 1934 and come directly under the British governor as a crown colony. Canada was proceeding with the development of universal healthcare, old-age pensions, and veterans' pensions. In 1948, the British government gave the people of Newfoundland the option to join Canada. In 1949, Newfoundland voted in favour of joining Canada as a province.

FORCED DISPLACEMENT OF INUIT FROM NUNAVIK – BROKEN PROMISES WITH INDIGENOUS PEOPLE

Canada decided to assert its territorial claims in the Arctic, leading to the relocation of the High Arctic. Several Inuit families were moved from Nunavik in Northern Quebec to Barren Cornwallis Island. In 1953 and 1956, the Inuit from Northern Quebec were relocated to Grise Fiord and Absolute Bay, now part of Nunavut. The government promised a more abundant place for the Inuit in which they could remain a united community. Additionally, the Inuit were promised the ability to leave and return to their home communities after two years if dissatisfied with the relocation.

The relocated Inuit had to cope with unfamiliar conditions and were left with no practical governmental support. They were taken from their home in Northern Quebec to the High Arctic, a region with a much colder climate, darker and longer winters, unfamiliar territory, and limited resources for survival. They lacked adequate shelter and supplies for survival and spent their first winter without enough food or resources. The Inuit were not provided with appropriate information about how different their lifestyle would be between their old homes and their new one. Upon arrival at their new location in the High Arctic, the Inuit were forcefully separated into two groups, dividing their families and communities.

Indigenous peoples continued living in oppression under the legacy of colonial governments. This forced displacement was a source of criticism of the government and was subjected to extensive investigation by the Royal Commission on Indigenous Peoples.

BIASED IMMIGRATION POLICY CHANGED

The restrictions on Canadian immigration were long in favour of the British and European immigrants due to inherent, systematic racism. These biased immigration policies started to change, and Canada started to consider more immigrants from developing countries. The 1950s in Canada saw high levels of immigration from Britain, Ireland, and Northern Continental Europe. Many racial discriminatory policies in Canada targeted Asian immigrants by charging head taxes, landing taxes, travel restrictions, and restrictions on Asian settlement. The new guidelines for removing racial discrimination from immigration policies were introduced. In 1967, a points system was introduced, eliminating racial discrimination from immigration policy.

After removing these discriminatory immigration policies, immigrants increasingly started to migrate from India, China, Vietnam, Jamaica, and Haiti in the 1970s. These newly immigrating individuals settled in the major urban centers, particularly Toronto and Vancouver, to join the much-needed workforce.

ATTEMPTED BOMBING OF CANADIAN PARLIAMENT

In May 1966, Paul Joseph Chartier carried a dynamite bundle and walked into the Parliament Building in Ottawa. These explosions erupted in a washroom of the chamber in which he managed to execute himself in the process. Chartier resorted to such a violent act to express how deeply he felt about MPs' regulation of the country. He was incredibly upset with their work. Supposedly, his goal was to execute as many members of the parliament as possible to save the country from people who he believed were unfit to run it. This was an expression of distrust in the Canadian democratic institution by Chartier.

CHAPTER 6

Pierre Trudeau Liberal Era (1968–79, 1980–84)

Prime Minister Pierre Trudeau was born in Outremont, Quebec, and served as the 15th Prime Minister of Canada from 1968 to 1984. He was the associate professor of law at the Université de Montréal. He joined the Liberal Party in 1965 and was elected to the House of Commons. He was appointed as Prime Minister Lester B. Pearson's parliamentary secretary. In 1967, he was appointed as minister of justice and attorney general. He liberalized divorce and abortion laws and decriminalized homosexuality in Canada. He won the Liberal leadership in 1968 and became Prime Minister of Canada after Lester B. Pearson. He also won the 1968, 1972, and 1974 elections. He lost the 1979 election but won shortly afterwards in 1980. He retired from politics shortly before the 1984 election. He won four elections with three majority governments and one minority government. He is the third-longest serving prime minister after William Mackenzie King and John A. Macdonald.

He maintained national unity amid the Quebec sovereignty movement and invoked the War Measures Act during the 1970 Quebec crisis. Quebec's proposal to seek sovereignty was overwhelmingly rejected in the

1980 Quebec referendum. He introduced the capital gains tax, deficit spending, oversaw the creation of Petro-Canada, and launched the National Energy Program in 1980. Throughout his political career, his goal in government was to make changes both socially and culturally. A few of his mandates included official bilingualism in Canada and multiculturalism. During Pierre Trudeau's tenure, the Canadian government adopted the world's first official multiculturalism policy.

Public Records

THE OFFICIAL LANGUAGE ACT

The Official Language Act declared English and French to be the official languages of Canada. The Act came into force in September 1969 under Prime Minister Pierre Trudeau's government. Both languages were of equal status in Canada and were provided in all the governmental services accessible to the public. The Official Language Act is the legislative foundation of Canada's Official Bilingualism. The Act was reintroduced as the Official Languages Act, which promoted the rights of all linguistic minorities.

The Royal Commission on Bilingualism and Biculturalism, established in 1963, made several recommendations, and the government responded by enacting the Official Language Act. The Official Language Act was enacted to ensure that federal government services would be offered in both official languages. At the time of the Act, less than 10% of federal governmental jobs were held by francophones. Over the years, jobs held by French-speaking populations have grown exponentially. The Official Language Act improved services in French and sought to bridge the divide between Canada's English- and French-speaking communities.

MULTICULTURAL POLICY

In 1971, Pierre Trudeau's government declared multiculturalism an official policy. The federal government of Canada has a responsibility to encourage a diverse society and the acceptance of all ethnicities and cultures. The government should be able to represent its society, including its diversity in religions, cultures, traditions, and languages. Canada was the first country in the world to develop such a policy. The Canadian Multicultural Act was set to ensure all Canadians were treated with equal respect by the government. The role of the Canadian government is to celebrate the diversity in its society and encourage it for its future generations. The act recognizes the rights of Indigenous peoples and minorities to embrace their cultures.

Canada was the first country to adopt multiculturalism as official legislation. This new policy, enforced across society, helped bridge gaps among several communities, including minority groups of different races, religions, and ethnicities. Societies began to become more multicultural as more individuals immigrated to Canada, contributing to the country's social and economic development. Most Canadians considered this a positive move to decrease the divide in the country.

OCTOBER CRISIS IN QUEBEC – CONTROVERSY OF THE WAR MEASURES ACT

An act of violence took place in October 1970 in the province of Quebec. Deputy Premier Pierre Laporte and British diplomat James Cross were kidnapped by the members of the Front de Libération du Québec (FLQ). LaPorte was found dead on October 17th, 1970. This heart-wrenching event led Prime Minister Pierre Trudeau to impose the War Measures Act in Quebec in October 1970. The War Measures Act gives the Canadian government broader powers over a province to maintain security during an act of war or violence. The act led to mass arrests, detentions without trials, and suspension of the liberties of people in Canada who may be perceived as "enemies". This Act was a federal law enacted after the commencement of World War I, and it also raised controversy and division in public opinion.

QUEBEC REFERENDUM – DIVISION OF THE FRENCH AND ENGLISH

In 1980, the first referendum was held on the issue of Quebec's sovereignty, followed by another in 1995.

Although the idea of independence was supported by a significant portion of the population, it was defeated, resulting in Quebec remaining part of Canada.

Though the first referendum in 1980 was defeated, the division in public opinion continued to ignite the sovereigntist movement, which pursued this idea once again. In 1995, the second referendum on sovereignty was held, in which the proposal for separation was once again rejected. The second referendum had a greater chance of resulting in a 'yes' victory for those who wanted sovereignty, with the 'no' side winning by 50.58%.

NATIONAL ENERGY PROGRAM – DIVISION AND OPPOSITION IN WESTERN CANADA

The National Energy Board (NEB), established in October 1980, took responsibility for authorizing imports and exports of oil and natural gas, and for setting tariffs and utility rates for oil pricing. It was responsible for the construction and performance of oil and pipelines across provincial and international borders. Prime Minister Pierre Trudeau announced the National Energy Program during his term, prompting opposition from the province of Alberta.

Oil prices had begun to rise; proponents believed the government needed to secure its oil resources to avoid an oil crisis that could affect the economy and the oil industry. For this reason, the National Energy Program was created to ensure that Canadian consumers were actively involved in the development of Canada's oil industry. Pierre Trudeau announced the program to take Canadian ownership of their oil and redistribute the wealth received by oil production to the federal government.

This objective sparked widespread controversy and opposition to the program in Western Canada. The provinces producing oil were opposed to this program. Premier Peter Lougheed of Alberta and opponents believed that such a significant policy change should have included consultation with provincial premiers, specifically those affected by the decision. Provinces believed it was unfair that the National Energy Program allowed the federal government to profit from the provinces' natural resources, thereby reducing provincial revenue. This issue caused a feeling of alienation in the Western provinces of Canada, including Alberta. Alienation grew as the Western provinces of Canada were exploited to benefit the Eastern provinces and the government.

CANADIAN CHARTER OF RIGHTS AND FREEDOMS

The Canadian Charter of Rights and Freedoms is an integral part of Canada's Constitution, enacted in 1982. The Charter establishes rights that apply to all citizens of Canada and to the government. The Charter was the last impactful act of Prime Minister Pierre Trudeau before his resignation in 1984. The rights and freedoms covered by the Charter include the right to equality, the freedom of speech and expression, the right to democratic government, and the legal rights of those accused of crime. All rights apply to everyone in Canada, including citizens and newcomers, but some sections of the Charter may apply only to citizens. The Canadian Charter of Rights and Freedoms protects all people in Canada against the state or government, subject to certain limitations.

Quebec is the only province in which the Canadian Charter of Rights and Freedoms does not "protect" and apply to minorities. After the legislation of Quebec's Bill 21, the dress code of minorities was dictated in the name of secularism.

BRITISH PARLIAMENT PASSES THE CANADA ACT 1982

In 1981, the Canadian House of Commons and Senate requested the enactment of the Act to end the British Parliament's power to legislate for Canada. On April 17, 1982, Queen Elizabeth II authorized the proclamation to bring the Constitution Act of 1982 into force. The Constitution Act led Canada into complete independence with Queen Elizabeth II as the nominal Monarch of Canada.

CHAPTER 7

Mulroney Conservative Era (1984-1993)

Martin Brian Mulroney served as the 18th prime minister of Canada from September 1984 to June 1993. He was born in Baie-Comeau, Quebec, in 1939. Before becoming prime minister, he was a lawyer in Montreal. In 1983, he became leader of the Progressive Conservatives and had a major victory in the 1984 federal election, winning in each province and territory. He got more than 50% of the votes for the first time since 1958 and 211 seats, the highest number of seats won by any party in Canadian history. He also won a second majority government in 1988.

Mulroney introduced many economic reforms, such as the Canada–United States Free Trade Agreement, the Goods and Services tax (GST), and the privatization of many Crown corporations, including Air Canada and Petro-Canada. He tried to seek Quebec's endorsement of the 1982 constitutional amendments by first introducing the Meech Lake Accord, followed by the Charlottetown Accord, but each of these accords failed to be ratified. He strengthened Canada's ties with the United States and made environmental protection a priority by signing a treaty with the United States on acid rain. He is appreciated for his role in opposing apartheid in South Africa. He was criticized for his response to the Air India Flight 182 bombing and his role in the resurgence of Quebec nationalism. He was also accused of corruption in the Airbus affair, a scandal that came to light only several years after he left office. Due to the decline in his popularity, he resigned in June 1993 when Kim Campbell became prime minister.

Public Records

AIR INDIA FLIGHT 182 BOMBING – DISREGARD OF CANADIANS OF INDIAN ORIGIN

June 23rd, 1985, marked the day Air India Flight 182 from Toronto to Delhi via Montreal and London was bombed. It exploded while travelling above the Atlantic Ocean, killing 329 passengers and crew members, most of whom were of Indian descent. The Royal Canadian Mounted Police (RCMP) launched an investigation to identify suspects who may have been involved.

Three men convicted of the bombing were members of a movement for an independent Sikh state in India after Operation Blue Star, an attack on the Sikh Golden Temple in India.

There was an abundance of controversy over whether the bombing was considered to be a Canadian tragedy, as the Canadian government did not declare it as one. Most of the people in the airplane were

Canadians of Indian origin going to India. Although most passengers were Canadian citizens, Prime Minister Brian Mulroney sent his condolences to Indian Prime Minister Rajiv Gandhi for India's loss. It seemed he did not consider the loss of Canadian citizens of Indian origin as a loss to Canada. Many families who were impacted by the bombing felt ignored by the government. Divisive policies and ignoring racial minorities only weaken Canada as a nation and encourage polarization and division in society.

DIVISION OF PUBLIC OPINION ON MULRONEY'S RELATION WITH THE US

Under the federal government of Brian Mulroney, the relationship between Canada and the United States became more defined. In 1989, the relationship between the two countries further developed as they signed the Free Trade Agreement. On March 13th, 1991, President Ronald Reagan of the United States of America and Prime Minister Brian Mulroney signed the Acid Rain Treaty. The Acid Rain Treaty was established between the US and Canada to organize action to tackle air pollution. In 1981, Canadians were protesting on Parliament Hill for the government to act against acid rain, as it was a top public issue in Canada.

A close relationship with the United States of America was concerning to the Canadian public, as it would have cultural and economic implications for

Canada. Despite their concerns, the government proceeded with the arrangement.

BRIAN MULRONEY'S FIGHT AGAINST SOUTH AFRICA'S APARTHEID

Brian Mulroney fought bravely against apartheid in South Africa. He pushed for economic sanctions against the South African regime in 1985-86 and demanded the end of the racist policies of the South African government. He stood for the release of Nelson Mandela and the elimination of apartheid without caring for the position of his allies, including Margaret Thatcher and Ronald Reagan. He played a major role in advocacy for the liberation movement and Nelson Mandela, who visited Canada in 1990. Mulroney was awarded the Order of the Companions of O.R. Tambo in 2015 for his great support for the country's liberation. Although some believe these actions came late and that Canada followed rather than led sanctions, Mulroney's role and advocacy were critical in modifying Western policies to ensure the peaceful transfer of power.

MEECH LAKE ACCORD – FAILURE OF MULRONEY'S EFFORT TO UNITE CANADIANS

The Meech Lake Accord, the result of a revised Canadian Constitution, was negotiated in 1987. The Meech Lake Accord included specific recognition of Quebec. Quebec had become an obstacle to achieving unity in Canada for decades. For the Accord to become law, it should have been ratified within the three-year time limit given to the federal government and all 10 Canadian provincial governments. The unanimous ratification must have been received by all provinces and territories in 1990 for the Accord to be in effect.

All provincial agreements to ratify the Accord were agreed upon by early June 1990. After all provinces agreed, concerns about the Accord were raised, causing ratification to fail in two provinces. Although the proposed amendment grew popular with citizens across Canada, concerns about the Accord led to a decline in its popularity. Thus, leading the Accord to its failure.

The failure of the Accord continued to boost the divide in Canada over constitutional matters. The tension between Quebec and the rest of the country continued. The second Quebec Referendum occurred in 1995. The referendum was a fight for Quebec's independence and, unlike the first referendum, had more citizens vote for Quebec to be a sovereign state. Despite support for the referendum, the idea still failed by a narrow margin.

OKA CRISIS – CONFLICT WITH INDIGENOUS PEOPLE

There has been a long history in Oka, Quebec, between the Mohawks and European settlers over the recognition of that land since the late 17th century. The Mohawks of Kanesatake wrote to government officials about the freedom of their community and their land, which was under the authority of the Sulpicians, a Roman Catholic order established by King Louis XV. This order declared that the Mohawk tribe be relocated and that their land be granted to the Sulpicians' mission. The Mohawk tribe relocated in hopes of gaining full ownership of their new territory, but that did not happen. Land rights were granted to European settlers, prompting the Mohawk community to fight for its land rights for over a century. Their rights to their land were repeatedly denied. By 1868, the government stripped Kanesatake of its status as a reserve belonging to Indigenous peoples.

By the end of World War II, only a 6-kilometre radius of Kanesatake was granted to the Mohawk community, now known as Oka.

In July 1990, the town of Oka decided to expand the neighbouring golf course and townhouses onto the territory of the Mohawk community of Kanesatake. This territory included the Mohawk burial ground, prompting the Mohawk community to refuse the council's order. This issue led to months of protests and high tensions among the Mohawk tribe, the Quebec police, the RCMP, and the army.

To halt construction on their territory, the Mohawk community in that area, along with activists from nearby areas, came together. They joined the protests, continuing to block roads and barricades. The provincial police force of Quebec was asked to intervene, prompting brief gunfire between the opposing parties. However, that did not stop the protests as supporters from across the country joined the Mohawk tribes at the barricades. The protests continued to grow, and the federal government became involved. The RCMP took their positions around the barricade, and soldiers from the Canadian Army joined to intervene. As tensions continued to grow, the Mohawk community united and fought for their land, regardless of the consequences.

The Mohawks staged their protests by blocking the road to the golf course, halting construction. Supporters continued to grow, prompting the government to call in Canadian forces to pressure the protesters. Soldiers took positions around the barricade with aircraft circling above. Negotiations lasted 78 days, and the resistance ended on September 26th, 1990. Over two and a half months of negotiations led to a deal. The federal government purchased the Pines, the site of the expansion, preventing future development on that land. The townhouses and golf course expansion were cancelled, and more land was purchased for the Kanesatake, reserved for the Mohawk community. This conflict led the federal government to understand the territorial rights of the Indigenous peoples. The tension gained international attention for First Nations rights and the Canadian Forces' approach to addressing the situation.

THE AIRBUS AFFAIR

The Airbus Affair was a scandal involving the acceptance of secret commissions as financial rewards for members of the Canadian government on Airbus plane sales to Air Canada. Complaints were made to the RCMP to investigate allegations that Prime Minister Mulroney engaged in misconduct and accepted kickbacks. After a two-year investigation, the inquiry concluded that former Prime Minister Mulroney acted inappropriately by accepting large cash payments. It was discovered that, shortly after his term as prime minister, Mulroney had accepted cash payments between 1993 and 1994. Mulroney was reported to have received three cash payments totalling at least $225,000.

In 2003, Mulroney reported accepting $225,000 and was still a member of parliament when he accepted one of the three payments. Mulroney argued that the money was paid to him for his consultation on international contacts. His claim was further investigated and found to have no supporting evidence. The money he accepted was not deposited into a bank account, nor were the payments disclosed or mentioned in a signed contract between the parties.

FIRST AND ONLY FEMALE PRIME MINISTER OF CANADA

Kim Campbell was Canada's first female prime minister after Prime Minister Brian Mulroney. She was selected to replace Brian Mulroney's office but lasted only a few months, as the Progressive Conservative Party suffered a defeat in 1993. As a result of their loss, she resigned.

63

CHAPTER 8

Jean Chrétien & Paul Martin Liberal Era (1993-2006)

Jean Chrétien was born on January 11th, 1934, in Shawinigan, Quebec. He served as the 20th prime minister of Canada from November 4th, 1993, to December 12th, 2003. He studied law at the University of Laval, Quebec. He was elected to parliament in 1963 and in many subsequent elections. He held various cabinet positions in the governments of Lester B. Pearson and Pierre Trudeau and was a Deputy Prime Minister of Canada for a few months in 1984 under John Turner. After John Turner resigned in 1990, Chrétien was elected as leader of the Liberal Party of Canada. In November 1993, the Liberal Party won the election with a majority government, and he became the prime minister of Canada. He was re-elected in both the 1997 and 2000 elections and served as prime minister of Canada for three terms.

Chrétien supported official bilingualism and multiculturalism. Additionally, Chrétien further developed the Youth Criminal Justice Act in Parliament in response to the growing number of youth in Canadian detention centers under the enforcement of the Young Offenders Act. Although he remained quite popular throughout his term as Prime Minister, he was occasionally subjected to controversies. He retired from politics in 2003 and is best known for promoting national unity against the movement of Quebec sovereignty.

Public Records

SPONSORSHIP SCANDAL

The Sponsorship Scandal involved the Canadian federal government's "Sponsorship Program." The Sponsorship Program initially raised the federal government's profile in Quebec. The objective of the program was to raise awareness of the federal government's contributions to Quebec to create a durable balance between Quebec and the other provinces of Canada.

The Sponsorship Program became a million-dollar scandal. The program was audited, uncovering the misappropriation of $ 100 million in federal funds and the misuse of public funds intended for government advertising in Quebec. The investigations showed the money had been used towards advertising firms to provide rewards and campaign funds for the Liberal Party in Quebec. This scandal negatively affected the Liberal brand in Quebec and across Canada for years, leading to a drop in Liberal poll numbers.

Prime Minister Paul Martin had to deal with the consequences of the scandal while insisting he had no role in it. He sided with the Canadian public, punishing those involved. The Prime Minister took action against anyone involved in the scandal to preserve the integrity of the Liberal Party. Several people involved in the program were fired, convicted, or ordered to repay specified amounts to the federal government.

SHAWINIGATE SCANDAL

The Shawinigate Scandal concerned the business deals of Prime Minister Jean Chrétien. He was accused of making real estate deals in Shawinigan, Quebec. In 1988, Chrétien bought a golf course and the Auberge Grande-Mere Hotel for $625,000 with two partners. Before he became the Prime Minister in 1993, he and his partners agreed to sell the hotel.

Jean Chrétien decided to sell his 25 percent share of the golf course to a businessman shortly after becoming prime minister. The buyer did not pay Chrétien until 1999, approximately 6 years after the agreement was made. Chrétien reported this to the Federal Ethics Counsellor, an institution of Parliament responsible for ensuring compliance with ethics and rules and handling conflicts.

Chrétien and his partners sold the hotel to another person who applied for a 2-million-dollar loan from the Business Development Bank of Canada to expand the hotel. Chrétien called the bank's director to support the loan's approval. Chrétien was seen as being in a conflict of interest for using his position to secure the loan for the new hotel owner.

In 1999, Prime Minister Jean Chrétien was accused of a conflict of interest. After an investigation, the Ethics Commissioner concluded that Chrétien had not violated any boundaries and was clear of wrongdoing. Chrétien won a third term in the 2000 federal election. Despite not facing consequences, Chrétien faced criticism from his opposing parties.

CANADA JOINED US-LED WAR IN AFGHANISTAN

Canada joined the Afghanistan war in October 2001 initially as part of a US-led coalition and later with a NATO-led mission. The 13-year war became Canada's longest war, which involved more than 40,000 personnel and resulted in 158 military personnel deaths. Canada ended its combat role in 2014, and this war cost an estimated $18 billion.

KYOTO ACCORD

The Kyoto Protocol is an international agreement that focuses on environmental issues and climate change. The protocol aimed to reduce carbon emissions and greenhouse gases in the atmosphere. As greenhouse gases threatened the global climate, the protocol was formed in Japan in 1997. Climate change became an important issue in Canada, leading the Liberal government to sign the Kyoto Protocol in 2002. The accord was nullified by Prime Minister Stephen Harper's Conservative government in 2007, in which

Prime Minister Stephen Harper was accused of muzzling the scientists.

CHRETIEN REFUSED TO JOIN THE US-LED IRAQ INVASION

In March 2003, Chrétien refused to join the US-led invasion of Iraq because of a lack of an explicit UN Security Council resolution authorizing force and proof of weapons of mass destruction. He preferred an independent foreign policy and the preservation of Canadian sovereignty. Chrétien believed that war was unnecessary and that Canadian soldiers should not participate in it. Despite friction with the U.S. President George W. Bush and criticism from some opposition parties, he did not give in. Canadian public opinion was divided on joining the war.

PAUL MARTIN WINS LIBERAL LEADERSHIP AND BECOMES PRIME MINISTER

Paul Martin was born in Windsor, Ontario, on August 28th, 1938. He served as the 21st prime minister of Canada. Paul Martin was a lawyer and was elected MP from the riding of LaSalle—Émard, Montreal in 1988. He ran for leader of the Liberal Party in 1990, losing to Jean Chrétien. Jean Chrétien appointed him as his minister of finance after the Liberal Party won a majority government in the 1993 federal election. He resigned as finance minister in 2002. He won the Liberal Party leadership in 2003 and became Prime Minister. In the 2004 federal election, the Liberal Party won a minority government. In 2005, the opposition parties passed a motion of no confidence in the House of Commons, which triggered the 2006 federal election and resulted in the Liberal Party's defeat.

CANADA'S CHRONIC FISCAL DEFICIT ELIMINATED.

When Paul Martin was appointed finance minister by Prime Minister Chrétien, Canada had one of the highest budget deficits among G7 countries. He made major budget cuts that slowed economic growth, leading to a loss of tax revenue. The Bank of Canada lowered interest rates, boosting economic growth and government revenue. Minister of Finance Paul Martin balanced the budget in 1998 after 29 years. He eliminated Canada's chronic fiscal deficit through his economic policies, which reduced spending and reformed many social programs.

SIGNING OF THE KELOWNA ACCORD

Paul Martin's government signed the Kelowna Accord to improve living conditions for Indigenous peoples. It was a 5.1-billion-dollar plan to improve Indigenous healthcare, education, and housing.

LEGALIZATION OF SAME-SEX MARRIAGE – DIVISION OF PUBLIC OPINION

On September 18th, 1995, the House of Commons voted and rejected the motion on same-sex marriage by 124 to 52, introduced by a homosexual MP. In 1999, the House of Commons overwhelmingly passed a resolution to reaffirm the definition of marriage as "the union of one man and one woman to the exclusion of all others." Paul Martin opposed same-sex marriage in a 1999 vote, as did most MPs. After various court rulings in 2003 and 2004 allowed for the legalization of same-sex marriages in seven provinces and one territory, his government proposed a bill to legalize same-sex marriage across Canada. The House of Commons passed the Civil Marriage Act in late June 2005.

The issue of same-sex marriage caused a division of public opinion. The divide on the issue across Canada was evident as thousands of people marched in demonstrations across the country, both for and against same-sex marriage.

Several polls were conducted, including one by Environics Research Group in March 2005, which was released just a few days before MPs were expected to vote on the bill introduced by the Liberal government. About 52 percent opposed the change in the definition of marriage to include same-sex couples, and 44 percent of respondents supported the legislation. Another 2005 opinion poll, conducted shortly before the Parliament legalized same-sex marriage, found that 42 percent of

Canadians favoured legalization, 40 percent were opposed, and the remainder did not respond.

CHAPTER 9

Harper Conservative Era
(2006-2015)

Stephen Joseph Harper served as the 22nd prime minister of Canada from 2006 to 2015. He was born in Toronto on April 30th, 1959. He withdrew from the University of Toronto and moved to Edmonton, Alberta, to work in the mail room at Imperial Oil. He earned a master's degree in economics in 1991 at the University of Calgary. Harper became a member of his high school's Young Liberals club but later joined the Progressive Conservative Party. He soon left the Progressive Conservative Party to join the Reform Party of Canada. Harper lost the 1988 federal election in Calgary West by a wide margin. He was first elected to the House of Commons in 1993 from Calgary. He did not seek re-election in 1997. He joined the National Citizens Coalition, a conservative lobbyist group. In 2002, he became the leader of the Canadian Alliance after Stockwell Day, the successor to the Reform Party, and returned to parliament as leader of the Official Opposition. In 2003, Harper successfully negotiated the merger of the Canadian Alliance with the Progressive Conservative Party of Canada to form the Conservative Party of Canada and was elected as the party's first leader in March 2004. The Conservative Party lost the 2004 federal election to the Liberal Party led by Paul Martin.

In the 2006 federal election, the Conservative Party won a minority government, and Harper became the prime minister of Canada. During his first term, his government faced the In and Out scandal, reduced the goods and services tax to five percent, and passed the Federal Accountability Act, the Québécois nation motion, and the Veterans' Bill of Rights. In the 2008 federal election, he again won a minority government. He prorogued Parliament to defeat a non-confidence motion by a potential coalition of opposition parties. He also passed the Economic Action Plan, which included major personal income tax cuts and infrastructure investments, during the Great Recession. He introduced the tax-free savings account and ordered military intervention during the First Libyan Civil War. In March 2011, a no-confidence vote found his government to be in contempt of Parliament, triggering a federal election in which he won a majority government with the New Democratic Party forming the Official Opposition for the first time. During his third term, Harper withdrew Canada from the Kyoto Protocol, privatized the Canadian Wheat Board, repealed the long-gun registry, passed the Anti-terrorism Act of 2015, and launched Canada's Global Markets Action Plan. He also faced the Canadian Senate expenses scandal and the Robocall scandal.

In the 2015 federal election, the Conservative Party lost to the Liberal Party, led by Justin Trudeau. Former Prime Minister Harper resigned his seat in August 2016. He was elected leader of the International Democracy

Union. He has been criticized for his policies against minorities, including Indigenous, Muslim, and Sikh communities of Canada; fearmongering and division, as well as the prorogation of Parliament four times for a total of 181 days. Only a summary of some of the Harper government scandals and major events in this era will be discussed below.

Public Records

CANCELLATION OF THE KELOWNA ACCORD – DISCRIMINATION AGAINST INDIGENOUS PEOPLE

After coming to power in 2006, Harper's Conservatives cancelled the Kelowna Accord. It was a 5.1-billion-dollar plan to improve Indigenous health care, education, and housing.

GUILTY PLEA ON AN IN AND OUT AFFAIR

The Harper Conservatives pleaded guilty to overspending in their 2006 campaign, violating the Elections Act. This resulted in an investigation conducted on the taxpayer's dime, during which over $ 2 million was spent.

HARPER'S DISRESPECT FOR FALLEN SOLDIERS

Harper's Conservative government refused to draw the Canadian flag at half-mast and banned media coverage in 2006 when Canadian soldiers' caskets from Afghanistan were being brought back to Canada. The family members of those fallen soldiers felt insulted, baffled, and disgusted by the lack of honour and respect shown to those who sacrificed their lives.

MP WAJID KHAN CROSSED FLOOR

Harper announced in January 2007 that Wajid Khan, Liberal MP from Mississauga-Streetsville, was crossing the floor. Khan was appointed as the PM's 'special adviser' on the Middle East and Afghanistan about six months ago while he was still in the Liberal caucus. Liberal leader Stephane Dion said that he wouldn't allow Wajid Khan to keep serving in the Tory post, as it was "bizarre" for a Liberal MP to serve both the opposition and the government and suggested that Khan should choose a side. Khan's floor crossing shifted the balance of power as Conservatives only needed the support of the 29-member NDP caucus to pass legislation. Harper took advantage of the Liberal Party's lack of a leader.

OBSTRUCTING THE COMMITTEE SYSTEM

The media reported in 2007 that Conservatives used strategies such as creating a handbook that directed committee chairpersons on how to obstruct the proceedings. These strategies also included barring witnesses, closure, time limitations and in-camera sessions.

DEVELOPMENT OF THE EQUALIZATION FORMULA TO WIN IN QUEBEC

Although the Harper Conservatives had strong support from Western Canada, they devised the equalization formula in 2007 to favour Quebec to win seats in the federal election. As a result, the Conservative government won multiple seats in the federal election. Alberta has always contributed to the equalization payment without receiving any amount. This later became one of the factors of the ongoing divide between Eastern and Western Canada when the Alberta economy began to suffer.

CUTTING FROM THE ESTABLISHMENT OF NATIONAL CHILDCARE

The Harper Conservative government cut 1.2 billion dollars in 2007 from the establishment of National Childcare, affecting many struggling families. These measures exacerbated the financial difficulties faced by Canadians living in poverty.

BLAMING SIKH MP TO HAVE A LINK WITH TERRORISM – DEMONIZING OF MINORITIES

In 2007, the Liberals opposed the Conservatives' plan to extend anti-terror legislation. Stephen Harper accused the Liberals and singled out Sikh MP Navdeep Bains for having a personal motive to protect MP Bains' father-in-law, Darshan Singh Saini. The Vancouver Sun had reported that Singh Saini was on a list of witnesses sought by Air India, but provided no proof of his involvement. The Liberals and MP Bains were offended in Parliament by the allegations made by Prime Minister Harper and urged the Prime Minister to apologize.

DENYING EXPATS THE RIGHT TO VOTE

In 1993, restrictions were introduced denying expats the right to vote if they had lived outside Canada for more than 5 years. These restrictions were not effectively enforced until 2007. Canadian expats residing abroad for more than five years were offended that the government infringed upon their right to vote as citizens.

CONSERVATIVES ABANDON THEIR OWN FIXED DATE ELECTION LAW

In 2008, Stephen Harper's government breached the law of having elections every four years. This was a law they had established, and after its violation, the legislation was terminated.

TORTURE OF AFGHAN DETAINEES

The Harper Conservative government refused to give Parliament documents related to the torture of Afghan detainees. Parliament wanted these documents to investigate whether Canada was involved in or aware of the torture of Afghan detainees after being returned to Afghan authorities. The investigation into the matter was halted as the Conservative government refused to disclose the documents. Canadian Diplomat Richard Colvin testified that Afghan detained individuals transported by Canadian forces were likely being tortured. The Conservatives disproved diplomat Richard Colvin's testimony because it shed more light on the wrongdoings. They decided to prorogue the Parliament in December 2009 to avoid criticism over the Afghan detainee issue.

FORMER CONSERVATIVE MP BROKE CONFLICT-OF-INTEREST RULES

Ethics Commissioner Mary Dawson released a report which disclosed Former Conservative MP Helena Guergis had broken ethical rules. In 2009, Guergis wrote a letter of recommendation to the town council of Simcoe, Ontario, in which she recommended a constituent's green-waste disposal company, Jim Wright's. Jim Wright had a business connection with her husband, Rahim Jaffer, a former Conservative MP.

CABINET STAFF IMMUNITY FROM TESTIMONY

The Harper Conservative government presented a new cabinet policy in 2010, directing that only cabinet ministers can appear as witnesses before parliamentary committees, excluding their political staff. They exempted their staffers from testifying before parliamentary committees.

CONTROVERSIAL APPOINTMENTS OF WATCHDOGS

The former Integrity Commissioner's office reviewed more than two hundred whistleblowing cases, but no meaningful disciplinary action followed. The former Integrity Commissioner was found to intimidate their employees, took punitive actions against them, and was paid over half a million dollars to leave office, as reported by the media in 2010.

REPEATED PROROGATION OF PARLIAMENT

Stephen Harper used prorogation of Parliament four times, for a total of 181 days, to avoid accountability. He used prorogation in 2010 to avoid the consequences of the Afghan detainees' file. It was the second prorogation the government took in one year.

PUTTING CONSERVATIVE PARTY LOGOS ON GOVERNMENT OF CANADA CHEQUES

The federal ethics commissioner told the Conservative government in 2010 that public spending announcements are not partisan matters and, therefore, should not be presented in that manner, as they are government activities. The Harper government made this a partisan activity by putting Conservative Party logos on cheques.

CUTTING FUNDING FOR WOMEN'S AND MINORITY GROUPS

There were huge cuts in the funding for women and minority groups by the Harper Conservative government in 2010. This tactic effectively prevented them from raising their voices and caused these groups to shut down 12 of their 16 established offices.

CONTEMPT OF PARLIAMENT

The Harper Conservative government was the first government in Canadian history to commit contempt of Parliament, as reported by the media in 2011. They withheld information on program costs that was rightfully presumed to be received by Parliament.

THE HOUSE OF COMMONS APPROVED THE MILITARY INTERVENTION IN LIBYA

In March 2011, the House of Commons authorized Canada's participation in the NATO-led mission of military intervention in Libya. Initially, Canada's involvement was for three months, but in June 2011, the House approved an extension of the mission. Canada played a major role in airstrikes, naval patrols, and the establishment of a no-fly zone. This mission lasted until October 31, 2011.

MISREPRESENTING THE REPORTS AND DOCUMENTS

The Harper Conservative government modified some of the writings and quotations in many documents produced by government agencies and officials. For example, the Harper government altered the CIDA document by Bev Oda's office on Kairos, as reported by the media in February 2011, the Senate Committee Report on the Mike Duffy scandal, and a report by former Auditor General Sheila Fraser on financial management.

CONSERVATIVE CRONIES IN IMPORTANT ROLES

In 2011, the media reported that a convicted person was appointed as a key advisor in the PMO. He used his position in the PMO to promote an eco-think tank and resigned from the PMO to manage it. He then transformed it into an oil industry booster with a 15 million dollars grant from the Harper Conservative government. He was involved in various other instances of illegal misconduct, given such opportunities through his connection to the Harper Conservative government.

USING 'HARPER GOVERNMENT' INSTEAD OF THE GOVERNMENT OF CANADA

The media reported in 2011 that the Conservative government directed public servants to use "Harper Government" instead of the "Government of Canada" in publicity releases. Internal memos disclosed by the Canadian Press uncovered that the Conservatives were the ones giving these orders when they originally rejected the involvement in this matter.

50 MILLION DOLLAR SPENDING MISMANAGEMENT AS DOCUMENTED BY THE AUDITOR GENERAL

The auditor general determined in 2011 that the government had misled Parliament and had spent $50 million on G8 summit-related vanity projects in Conservative Minister Tony Clement's riding of Parry Sound-Muskoka. This money was originally reserved for infrastructure projects.

MINISTER SLASHES CBC BUDGET

After the 2011 federal elections, Heritage Minister James Moore stated that his party would either advance or maintain their support for CBC. The following year, the Conservatives reversed their promise and made the biggest cut to the CBC since the mid-1990s.

CONSERVATIVES ROBOCALLS SCAM

A conservative campaign worker in Guelph was imprisoned for his role in the Robocalls Scam. On polling day, May 2nd, 2011, hundreds of calls purporting to be from Elections Canada and giving erroneous poll information were made in the riding of Guelph to the voters who did not support the Conservative Party. The Council of Canadians brought a case, and another court ruled that the scam was widespread and not limited to the Guelph riding.

THE PASSING OF JACK LAYTON, LEADER OF THE OPPOSITION

Leader of the New Democratic Party and Leader of the opposition, Jack Layton, died on August 22, 2011, from cancer. He led the NDP from thirty-seven to 103 during the 2011 federal election.

HARPER DECLARES ISLAMISM THE GREATEST THREAT TO CANADA

Stephen Harper said in an interview with the CBC in September 2011 that the biggest security threat to Canada is Islamic terrorism, a decade after 9/11. He said Canada is safer than it was on September 11th, 2001, when al-Qaeda attacked the US, but that "the major threat is still Islamism." He also stated, "There are other threats out there, but that is the one that I can tell you occupies the security apparatus most regularly in terms of actual terrorist threat." He mentioned that terrorist threats can "come out of the blue" from a different source, such as the recent Norway attacks, where a lone gunman who hated Muslims killed seventy seven people. He said terrorism by Islamic radicals is still the top threat, though a "diffuse" one.

CAMPAIGN AGAINST MP

The Conservative speaker of the House, Andrew Scheer, made remarks about how it was unacceptable for his party to be acting secretly with the misinformation that took place in MP Irwin Cotler's riding. The MP stated in November 2011 that he had made phone calls to his constituents to ask whether they would support the Conservative Party in the by-election. These misleading calls gave the constituents the impression that he was resigning. This had a negative impact on his relationship with his constituents and interfered with his ability to discharge his functions as an MP.

CONSERVATIVES ATTEMPT ELECTION CAMPAIGN FRAME-UP

During the 2011 election campaign, Harper accused Michael Ignatieff of being an Iraq war planner. Neither the Conservatives nor the media attempted to verify the story's truth when it was published.

CITIZENS EJECTED FROM CONSERVATIVE RALLIES

Stephen Harper's campaign organizers kicked citizens out of their campaign rallies in 2011 on suspicion of affiliation with opposing political parties. A spokesperson for Harper apologized for this behaviour.

MINISTERS RECKLESS SPENDING OF TAXPAYERS MONEY

International Development Minister Bev Oda visited London in June 2011. The Canadian Press report disclosed Oda had rebooked her hotel at the Swanky Savoy Hotel, which cost her approximately $665 per night, rather than staying at the hotel where the conference was taking place. The total bill for her three-day stay, including the room and room service, was $1,995. Additionally, Oda hired a car and driver for approximately $1,000 per day to bring her to the hotel where the conference was held, the same hotel where she was originally booked. She also incurred a cancellation charge for not staying at the Grange St. Paul's Hotel. This was just one example of reckless spending of taxpayers' money.

COMPANIES MAKING ILLEGAL DONATIONS TO CONSERVATIVE CANDIDATES

Former Conservative MP for Labrador Peter Penashue resigned in 2013 amid allegations regarding his 2011 election. His 2011 election campaign raised allegations that it had accepted twenty-eight illegal contributions from various corporations. Penashue then reimbursed the government $30,000 for the illegal contributions he accepted from corporations. Penashue's campaign had spent approximately 21% over its campaign limit, according to CBC News. He claimed to have been unaware of these contributions and stated that it was a mistake by a volunteer who filed the Elections Canada return for his 2011 campaign.

JOHN BAIRD, TONY CLEMENT AND LAURIE HAWN'S GOLD-EMBOSSED BUSINESS CARDS

In 2011, in his new role as Foreign Affairs Minister, John Baird ordered gold business cards, requesting that the Canadian logo and his place of employment be removed. These cards were in violation of the Treasury Board Policy. The Treasury Board of Canada administers government spending to confirm tax dollars are being spent wisely. John Baird's orders opposed the Treasury Board, but he still prevailed by getting his gold-embossed business cards. Following in his footsteps, Tony Clement, Treasury Board President in the May 2011 Cabinet, received gold cards along with Laurie Hawn, Edmonton MP, who was temporarily a member of the cabinet committee. These cards violated several policies, including having unilingual gold cards and featuring Canada's coat of arms, coloured gold, visible on the card. While Clement and Hawn claimed this was an error and reimbursed the government through their personal accounts, Baird did not follow suit. He defended his cards, recognizing that they violated Canadian rules, and ordered a second set of bilingual cards.

MINISTER VIOLATED CONFLICT-OF-INTEREST RULES IN A MILLION-DOLLAR FUNDING TO A COMMUNITY CENTRE

Diane Finley, Minister of Public Works, was proven to have worked improperly by the ethics commissioner. Finley had violated the Conflict-of-Interest Act by funding $1 million to build a Jewish Community Centre in Markham, Ontario, in 2011. The project was backed by Rabbi Chaim Mendelsohn, a close acquaintance of Conservative Minister John Baird. Mary Dawson released a report stating that Rabbi Mendelsohn's application to the fund had been rejected, but the rejection was overruled by Minister Finley after John Baird spoke to her about the funding. Prime Minister

Stephen Harper defended Minister Finley's action despite her violating various policies.

FORMER CABINET MINISTER BROKE CONFLICT-OF-INTEREST RULES, HELPING "FACILITATE ACCESS" FOR HIS WIFE AND HER EMPLOYER

The ethics commissioner stated that section 33 of the Conflict of Interest Act prohibits public office holders from taking advantage of their previous office. Jay Hill violated section 33 of the act in 2011 by reaching out to the ministers he had worked with before leaving politics in 2010. He reached out to them to inform them about a multinational energy deal, in which his wife and her employer were parties, as they had written the communications plan for it. The ethics commissioner concluded her investigation by finding that Jay had, in fact, reached out to his former colleagues to aid his wife.

JASON KENNY BANS NIQAB

In December 2011, Immigration Minister Jason Kenny unilaterally imposed a ban on the wearing of the niqab while taking the oath of citizenship. Prior to then, Muslim women were allowed to wear a niqab or burqa during the ceremony and recite the oath. This change led to women who wear a niqab being unable to become Canadian citizens. Human rights advocates dismissed the issue of identity verification, arguing that immigration officers could confirm the identities of such women.

DECLINING TO SHARE BUDGET INFORMATION

The Harper Conservative government refused the PBO's request to provide details of the cuts in the 2012 federal budget, to analyze their impact on social services and programs. The Harper Conservative government declined to explain why it had cut funding for Canada's independent watchdog, mocking parliament's right to control the public purse, despite having lost a court case and being ordered to comply with the rules.

COSTING OF F-35 FIGHTER JETS

A 2012 report by the auditor general revealed that the Conservatives misled the public and Parliament about the estimated cost of the fighter jet procurement project.

BLAMING STATS CANADA FOR KILLING THE LONG FORM CENSUS

The Conservative government cancelled the long-form census, and according to Industry Minister Tony Clement, Statistics Canada supported this decision. He stated that the new form the government was developing would bring similar statistical data. However, Statistics Canada confirmed in 2012 that it had never supported the Conservatives' decision.

CONSERVATIVE GOVERNMENT SUED BY WHISTLEBLOWER

Harper Conservatives frequently introduced bills that were rejected by the courts. Many critics suggested that Harper used these opportunities to make political statements, rather than investing his time and resources in implementing effective policies. As reported by the media in December 2012, a senior member of the Justice Department was so displeased with Harper's constant, immature acts of introducing inadmissible bills that he decided to sue the government for breaking the law and introducing legislation that infringed the Charter of Rights and Freedoms. He was suspended without pay and justification.

INTERFERENCE WITH INDEPENDENT AGENCIES

Harper's government interfered with agencies such as the National Energy Board, as reported by the media in 2012. Furthermore, the independence of the Canadian Radio-Television and Telecommunications (CRTC) was also substantially affected. The government targeted the Parliamentary Budget Office with criticism and budget cuts for its critical reporting on government spending.

GOVERNMENT MUZZLING SCIENTIFIC COMMUNITY

It was reported in 2012 that the Harper Conservative government ordered "media minders" to keep a close eye on the scientists who worked for Environment Canada and report on them. This led scientists to organize the "Death of Evidence" protests as their freedom of expression was being infringed upon.

REPRESSION OF RESEARCH REPORTS

Harper Conservatives concealed reports, documents, and research, such as a Firearms Report, from the public during a gun registry debate, as reported by the media in 2012. This was done by the government to pursue its own partisan agenda.

THE PORNO SMEAR OF POLITICAL OPPONENTS

In 2012, the Minister of Public Safety, Vic Toews, suggested that anyone who disputed the government's decision on electronic surveillance of Canadians by authorities was on the same side as child pornographers.

BLANKET SURVEILLANCE OF PROTESTERS

The Conservative government authorized an operation wherein all advocates, protestors, and demonstrators can be monitored by the authorities. A leaked memo also revealed that the Harper government asked other federal departments and agencies to help them compile a comprehensive list of protestors, demonstrations, and advocates. CSIS held significant power, but the government decided to grant it even more power without any justification. A security specialist stated that this infringes on Canadians' rights and freedoms as set out in the Charter of Rights and Freedoms. The government was reported to have spent more than $ 20 million on media-monitoring contracts since December 2012.

CURBING OF RIGHTS AND DISMANTLING OF GROUPS

A Montreal-based group, Rights and Democracy, was knocked down because of their political affiliations, as reported by the media in April 2012. The Harper Conservative government also demolished other organizations for having political affiliations with opponents, such as the church group Kairos, whose funding was cut. In addition, the head of the Nuclear Safety Commission was also dismissed for an affiliation with an opposition party long ago.

VETERANS' ADVOCATES SMEAR CAMPAIGN

Several weeks of internal investigation, as reported by the media in February 2012, found that many bureaucrats were found guilty of leaking medical and psychiatric details of a retired Canadian Forces captain.

STRIPPING HEALTHCARE FROM REFUGEES

The Harper government in 2012 decided to deny health care to refugees, for whom a federal court had ruled it was "cruel and unusual." According to the article, an internal poll commissioned by Citizenship and Immigration Canada (CIC) suggested that 62% of Canadians agreed that refugees should have access to the same health care benefits as Canadian citizens.

SENATOR'S EXPENSES

There were reports that the senators submitted 150 expense claims to the Senate, and some claims for the same expenses were submitted twice, in 2009 and 2012. The investigators believed the senator committed fraud and breach of trust.

PRESSURING THE RCMP TO DESTROY LONG-GUN REGISTRY DATA

The RCMP had destroyed long-gun registry data after receiving pressure from cabinet ministers, government officials, and Prime Minister Stephen Harper. Parliament passed a law in 2012 to end long-gun registries, and while there was still one last request for the information, the RCMP opposed the law by destroying the records related to the last request. Guaranteed by subsection 4 of the Access to Information Act, those records were entitled to access, which the RCMP was aware of, yet it proceeded to destroy them. Suzanne Legault advised a charge against the RCMP for deliberately destroying the document protected under the Access to Information Act.

LABELLING ENVIRONMENTALISTS AS "RADICALS"

In 2012, Federal Minister of Natural Resources Joe Oliver described environmentalists and climate change activists as "radical groups" who were halting projects and opportunities for the oil, metal, gas, and mineral industries to produce and expand their operations. He claimed that environmentalists were a threat to the regulatory system, pursuing their own personal agenda. Oliver continued to accuse environmentalists of using their ideologies to delay projects and exploit the system.

INDUSTRY MINISTER BREAKING CONFLICT-OF-INTEREST RULES BOOSTING JAFFER'S BUSINESS INTERESTS

The Conflict-of-Interest Act is in place to ensure that ministers are using their powers fairly. Industry Minister Christian Paradis was reported to have broken the law when he provided favourable treatment to former MP Rahim Jaffer in March 2012. Mary Dawson declared that Paradis' actions were in good faith. Jaffer had approached Paradis, in charge of public works, with a proposal on behalf of his company, Green Power Generation. The proposal opted for solar panels, and Paradis had helped Jaffer in securing meetings with

Public Works officials. Dawson concluded that their previous relationship may have been a factor in the decision-making process, but Rahim Jaffer's proposal was a credible idea, effective enough to advance.

FORMER FINANCE MINISTER BREAKING CONFLICT-OF-INTEREST RULES

Finance Minister Jim Flaherty violated the conflict-of-interest code as he used his minister title in a letter sent on March 30th, 2012, to Canada's broadcast regulator to influence their decision in picking radio station applications. Flaherty used his position to bring support to a radio station application submitted to Canada's broadcast regulator on behalf of a company operating in his riding. He accepted responsibility for the inappropriateness of including his ministerial title in the letter, and the ethics commissioner ruled that similar letters will not be allowed in the future without her office's approval.

MISUSING OFFICIAL RESIDENCES ABROAD

John Baird had been accused of misusing overseas residences available to him. John Baird had taken a group of friends to New York for five days, residing in the official residence of Canada's Consul-General for the New Year's holidays in 2012. In 2013, he was seen with a group of friends staying in London for eight days at the Canadian High Commissioner's. While the opposition criticized Baird for residing abroad on public funds, his office noted that taxpayers did not fund these trips. The owners of both residences where Baird resided were personal friends of the minister and had offered them to Baird. However, the opposition still criticized Baird's trips, arguing that it was inappropriate for a government official to vacation without paying for it and to invite friends to join him. Minister Baird said he had paid for all other accommodations for the trips, but the NDP foreign affairs critic, Paul Dewar, argued that Mr. Baird should disclose his friends to confirm they are not political donors.

ELIMINATING THE CANADIAN WHEAT BOARD

In 1935, the Canadian Wheat Board was an organization established to control the purchase and export of Canadian wheat and barley. In August 2012, the Harper government terminated the Canadian Wheat Board's "single desk" model and opened the market, allowing companies to raise their market share. While many farmers in the industry were joyous over this elimination, former directors of the Canadian Wheat Board argued that more wealth could be driven away from farmers.

SPENDING 2.5 MILLION DOLLARS PROMOTING A PROGRAM THAT DOES NOT EXIST

The federal government advertised online and in television commercials to publicize a training program that had not yet been established at the time of the promotion. In 2013, the federal government spent 2.5 million dollars through Employment and Social Development Canada to advertise the Canada Job Grant, which had not yet started because the federal government needed provincial agreement. The training program took effect in 2014, one year after the program's advertisements. The opposition criticized the federal government for wasting money on promoting a program that had not yet been implemented.

PMO STAFF AND SENATE MONEY SCANDAL

The prime minister's office staffers were reported to be involved in making secret payments to senators for political reasons. Media outlets also reported in 2013 on the Senate expenses scandal, which brought forward many more unethical stories. PMO's staff was also involved in altering the Deloitte audit. There were allegations of a cover-up, misconduct that resulted in the breaking of public trust, and the whitewashing of a Senate report.

RESTRICTIONS PLACED ON MEDIA ACCESS

Harper's government imposed restrictions on journalists, limiting their ability to perform their duties and infringing upon their rights. The Conservatives' 2013 Calgary convention was an instance where the journalists were being harassed and mistreated by the PMO's staff. Mark Bourrie, a journalist, wrote in his book, Killing the Messenger, about the new limits imposed in the Harper era that restricted reporters' freedom of speech.

HARPER GOVERNMENT SPYING ON INDIGENOUS CRITIC, 'RETALIATED'

Cindy Blackstock was monitored by the government as she was an Indigenous child welfare advocate, as reported in May 2013. When she visited the Ministry of Aboriginal Affairs for a meeting with other First Nations leaders, Blackstock was the only one denied entry. A staff member from the Ministry misbehaved with her. The Canadian Human Rights Tribunal awarded her $20,000 for the mental abuse and psychological suffering she endured from that event.

ELECTION VIOLATIONS LEADING TO THE RESIGNATION OF A CABINET MEMBER

Peter Penashue, who also supported the Harper Conservative government, had to resign from the campaign in 2013 due to election spending violations.

CONSERVATIVE SENATORS MOONLIGHTING AS CONSERVATIVE FUNDRAISERS

Many senators became involved with political fundraising for the Conservatives, and some were entangled in scandals, charged with breach of trust, or faced lengthy court battles. Claude Carignan, appointed by Harper in 2008 as a Conservative Senator, was identified as fundraising for the Conservative Party. In 2013, Patrick Brazeau attended a fundraising dinner for Conservative candidate Andrew Lister in Ontario. Marjory LeBreton, leader of the Senate in 2014, attended a fundraising breakfast as its "featured guest."

CONSERVATIVE SENATOR BREAKING CONFLICT-OF-INTEREST RULES

Senator Pierre-Hugues Boisvenu had violated the conflict-of-interest code by pursuing a relationship with Isabelle Lapointe, the executive assistant he had hired in 2010. When their relationship became public in 2013, Lapointe was appointed to seek employment outside the Senate. She asked for two weeks' leave before starting a new job to avoid the media's attention. Boisvenu took it upon himself to make sure she got the two weeks' leave.

FORMER CONSERVATIVE MP BREAKING CONFLICT OF INTEREST RULES

Mississauga-Brampton MP Eve Adams had been accused of violating conflict of interest rules in a similar manner to Finance Minister Jim Flaherty. She wrote a letter to the Canadian Radio-Television and Telecommunications Commission, signing it as MP and Parliamentary Secretary to the Minister of Veterans Affairs, as reported by the media in January 2013. The letter was written to support a radio station in Brampton, Ontario. According to the Ethics Commissioner, including this title was unacceptable and constitutes a breach of Conflict-of-Interest rules.

JUSTIN TRUDEAU WINS LEADERSHIP OF LIBERAL PARTY

In April 2013, Justin Trudeau won the Liberal leadership held in Ottawa. He was going to lead the third-place party into the 2015 federal election. He was an MP from the riding of Papineau, Montreal. He received almost 80 percent of the votes on the first ballot.

STATEMENT MADE BY CONSERVATIVE CABINET MINISTER ABOUT CHILD POVERTY IN CANADA

In 2013, Senior Conservative Cabinet Minister James Moore was questioned about what the federal government could do in response to Canada's child poverty statistics. In 2013, one in every seven Canadian children lived in poverty. He responded that child poverty was not the government's problem or responsibility. He later apologized for the comment he made after receiving severe criticism from opposition parties and the public.

PETER MACKAY SAYS THE HOMELESS SHOULD PAWN THEIR BELONGINGS TO PAY FOR COURT FINES

In a December 2013 interview, former Justice Minister Peter MacKay argued that homeless people should sell their belongings to pay the mandatory surcharge if convicted of an offence. The Conservative Government removed judges' ability to waive fees for offenders unable to pay the penalty for their crimes. The surcharge was brought into force, and a mandatory surcharge was introduced for offences. Judges created different options for homeless people, such as extending the time to pay fines.

MP MISLEADING THE PARLIAMENT

Conservative MP Brad Butt was reported by the media in 2014 to have said that he observed voter cards being misused. Many opposition MPs called on the government, suggesting that it was "rigging the elections in their favour." However, Mr. Butt stood in the House weeks later and said that his claims were false. He apologized but failed to explain what he had said initially.

HOUSE LEADER ADMITS TO MOCKERY

MP Paul Calandra, who was the Parliamentary Secretary to Harper, made a heartfelt apology in the House in September 2014 for abusing the democratic process after Opposition MPs criticized and demanded answers from the government.

HARPER ACCUSED THE SUPREME COURT CHIEF JUSTICE

In May 2014, Stephen Harper accused the Chief Justice of the Supreme Court of Canada of misconduct after his nominees' appointments were rejected for ineligibility. When the evidence was reviewed, it contradicted his claims against the Chief Justice.

CONSERVATIVE MPS PROTEST MUZZLING

In 2014, some parliamentarians stood up to confess that they had been prevented from disclosing information by the Prime Minister's Office during question period. Former Conservative backbencher Brent Rathgeber decided to sit as an independent and published a book, *Irresponsible Government*, condemning their anti-democratic practices.

CLOSING OF AQUATIC SCIENCE LIBRARIES

Harper Conservatives significantly reduced the number of federal libraries in 2014 by abruptly closing seven globally well-known Department of Fisheries and Oceans archives. No valid or logical reasoning was provided for the government's decision to close these educational institutions. A leaked memo described this as a "book burning," as it inhibited and limited access to environmental resources and information. The Harper government disclosed that the information would be retained digitally but failed to provide a plan on how it would be executed. The scientists believed that digitizing the information could not replace the work that was lost.

REVENUE CANADA'S ATTACK ON SELECTED CHARITIES

Some charities that advocated for human rights and free speech were increasingly targeted by the Canada Revenue Agency. A left-leaning think tank raised concerns about the possibility of political interference in audits of charities in October 2014. Many charities that did not conform to the Harper Conservative government's policies and were at risk of being targeted joined forces to push back against a politically motivated witch-hunt.

CONSERVATIVES RUN UNDERCOVER STING OPERATIONS

The Conservatives had conducted undercover sting operations against their opponents to entrap them. For instance, a sting operation against a Liberal candidate in Banff-Airdrie was supported by then-Harper Conservative employment minister, as reported by the media in November 2014.

PMO DEPLOYS INTERNS FOR DIRTY TRICKS

The Harper Conservatives disrupted Justin Trudeau's speech by using a tactic similar to one former US President Richard Nixon used, as reported by the media in 2014. They sent junior PMO staffers, disguised as ordinary people, to interrupt the event.

CONSERVATIVE ELECTIONS BILL TO STRIP POWER FROM ELECTIONS CANADA

The Fair Elections Act, introduced in February 2014 by the Harper Conservatives, made it more difficult for Canadians to vote by requiring additional identification. This led Pierre Poilievre to retract some of the rules implemented following a nationwide protest, in which more than 400 academics took part and called on the government to make changes.

MINISTER SMEARS HEAD OF ELECTIONS CANADA

Democratic Reform Minister Pierre Poilievre blamed Elections Canada's CEO in 2014 for being a power-monger and for wearing a team jersey as a strategy to challenge his integrity and defame him.

COPYRIGHT GRAB FOR ATTACK ADS

CTV News reported in October 2014 that the Tories wanted to rewrite copyright laws to allow political parties to grab content from the media and use it for free in their ads. CTV suggested that MPs, commentators, and reporters would have to be careful about what they say, as it could backfire, especially if used in a political attack. It was stated that the Harper Conservative government "could be seen flirting with fascism."

SENATORS AND LACK OF TRUST

In 2014, Senator Patrick Brazeau and former Senator Mac Harb were charged with one count of fraud and breach of trust. These charges were administered by the RCMP for fraudulent activity related to Senate expenses. In October of 2014, Senator Patrick Brazeau was suspended from the Senate, along with Senators Mike Duffy and Pamela Wallin, of the Conservative Party. Liberal Senator Mac Harb retired earlier in August of 2014 after repaying $ 231,000 in expenses. Brazeau, Duffy, and Wallin were investigated regarding their expense claims, which they were not entitled. Duffy was charged with 31 counts of breach of trust, bribery, and fraud. Duffy was then freed from his charges and rejoined the Senate in April of 2016. Wallin was not charged after a 3-year investigation. Charges against Brazeau and Harb were dropped, allowing Brazeau to return to the Senate.

PAUL CALANDRA'S RESPONSE IN PARLIAMENT

MP Calandra apologized in the House of Commons for responding to questions about Iraq in ways unrelated to the topic. MP Paul Calandra was questioned by NDP Leader Thomas Mulcair in 2014 regarding more information about Canada's recent strike in Iraq. To redirect attention away from Canada's military mission in the Middle East, Paul Calandra responded with a series of accusations toward the NDP and their failure to support Israel. Mulcair approached Andrew Scheer to demand that Calandra answer the questions, which was a rule of the House. Scheer ignored Mulcair's request, resulting in Calandra and various other Tory MPs receiving criticism from the opposition.

LEONA AGLUKKAQ IGNORES QUESTIONS ABOUT PEOPLE IN HER RIDING

During a question period in December 2014, Environment Minister Leona Aglukkaq was reading a newspaper while opposition members questioned her about residents in her riding searching for food in a landfill. The North was facing a significant food crisis, as the Conservatives' Nutrition North Program failed to deliver effective results for residents. Aglukkaq tried to settle the situation by informing CBC News that it was part of Northern culture not to waste food, and that people may have been searching for food to salvage from landfills to preserve it. She publicly apologized for her poor judgment in reading the newspaper during the question period to find information regarding people searching for food in her riding. Amid an ongoing food crisis across Canada, particularly in the North, Aglukkaq's response to such crises was seen as insensitive and ineffective, as she framed it as a normal occurrence and as something within their "culture" not to waste food.

JOHN WILLIAMSON BILLS TAXPAYERS

Conservative MP John Williamson attended the Canadian Taxpayers' Federation Conference in Vancouver, BC, in 2014. The purpose of the conference was to invite conservatives from across the globe to discuss new ideas that could support government accountability. Ironically, John Williamson had funded his trip to the conference at the taxpayers' expense. The House of Commons documented Williamson's expenses, which totalled nearly $3,000 and were billed to taxpayers.

CONSERVATIVE CANDIDATE PHOTOBOMBS TAXPAYER-FUNDED EVENTS

In August 2014, Conservative Candidate Tim Laidler won the nomination in his riding of Port Moody-Coquitlam. After his win, Tim Laidler was seen at various Government of Canada events, standing alongside Conservative Ministers. Pictures taken at these publicly funded events by Laidler were used on his social media to generate publicity.

NAMING AN ENBRIDGE LOBBYIST TO OVERSEE CSIS

Former Conservative Cabinet Minister Chuck Strahl resigned from his position on the Security Intelligence Review Committee in 2014 amid questions about his lobbying for Enbridge, the company seeking to build a pipeline between Alberta and British Columbia. Although it was not a conflict of interest for him to serve as chair of SIRC while lobbying for Enbridge, it put him in a difficult position, making him the center of controversy.

LAUNCHING AUDITS ON ENVIRONMENTAL GROUPS

In 2014, the Canada Revenue Agency conducted thorough audits of seven of Canada's most prominent environmental groups to confirm that their advocacy complied with the CRA's guidelines. Exceeding these restrictions set by the CRA could result in a termination of their charitable status. Environmental organizations were under surveillance by the Conservative government through an increasing number of audits. Many of these environmental groups were critics of the Conservative government and felt they faced bias because of their criticism.

SPENDING HALF A BILLION DOLLARS TO CREATE ONLY 800 JOBS

In 2014, the Conservative government's Small Business Job Credit created approximately eight hundred jobs. The Job Credit took over $500 million from the Employment Insurance fund, giving $ 687,500 to each of the 800 jobs created. The money was withdrawn from the Employment Insurance Fund, and the Employment Insurance premium freeze, which occurred simultaneously, resulted in approximately 10,000 jobs being eliminated. The Conservative job creation plans left Canadians with even fewer jobs.

PETER MACKAY SENT FEMALE JUSTICE DEPARTMENT STAFF PATRONIZING MOTHER'S DAY EMAILS

In 2014, Former Justice Minister Peter MacKay was put in the spotlight over allegations that he made sexist comments. The first incident concerned an allegation that MacKay insinuated there were fewer female judges because they feared the occupation would take time away from their children. He denied the allegation but remained under scrutiny when the Department of Justice staff received emails for Mother's Day and Father's Day. The emails included sexist comments, thanking mothers for their duty in "changing diapers," while fathers were appreciated for their role in shaping the next generation. He claimed not to have written that email; the email was written by a female Justice Official to whom he signed off.

DEFENDING THE RCMP AGAINST POTENTIAL CRIMINAL CHARGES

In 2015, the media reported that the Conservative government protected the RCMP from accountability by reinstating an old bill before it was approved by Parliament.

MINISTER'S ADVERTISING SCAM WITH TAXPAYERS' MONEY

In 2015, the Globe and Mail reported that Stephen Harper's Minister for Democratic Reform, Pierre Poilievre, used public servants on overtime to film him at a Sunday meeting with constituents. The Minister used taxpayers' money to create vanity videos.

ACCESS TO THE INFORMATION SYSTEM BLOCKED

Stephen Harper's Conservative Government created many obstacles, as the former Information Commissioner noted in his 2015 conclusion, which was reported by the media. He suggested that since the prime minister gained "absolute power," the prime minister "has absolutely abused that power to the maximum."

MISTREATMENT OF IMMIGRANTS

The United Nations Rights Committee reported in July 2015 that the changes the Harper government made to Canada's immigration and refugee system were despicable. These changes caused mental torture, which migrants had to endure as they were being detained and incarcerated without due process.

PMO COVERING UP VIDEO LEAK PUTTING TROOPS AT RISK

A security breach was reported in May 2015, where the Conservative government inappropriately published photos of Canadian soldiers posted in Iraq. The PMO was trying to cover up a promo video that was disclosed.

HUGE PARTISAN POLITICAL ADVERTISING WITH TAXPAYER MONEY

Several media reports disclosed in 2015 that the Harper Conservative government spent over $750 million on partisan political advertising funded by taxpayer money. Some examples of where Harper's government wasted taxpayers' money include ads promoting a jobs grant program. Harper's government decided to air the ad without presenting it to Parliament or the other provinces. Secondly, Harper targeted Justin Trudeau via an email blast, using taxpayers' money.

CONSERVATIVES PROVIDED THEIR OWN RIDINGS WITH INFRASTRUCTURE FUNDS

It was reported in July 2015 that Conservatives ensured that more than 80 percent of the infrastructure fund projects go to their own ridings.

HARPER'S PATRONAGE APPOINTMENTS

Prime Minister Harper discarded the Public Appointments Commission and, in June of 2015, made 98 patronage appointments. This included filling various positions with the loyalists before the election.

BANNING THE JOURNALISTS FOR ASKING QUESTIONS

A journalist was covering Harper's speech on oil to a business audience. He asked a question about the charges laid against a Conservative MP. PMO tried to ban him and his network from covering Harper's trip to Malaysia, but failed to do so after the word circulated. As reported by the media in June 2015, the PMO was demanding that journalists attending any Harper press conference put their names on a list, so it could pick and choose who got a chance to ask questions.

CONSERVATIVES PUSH TO FORCE THROUGH ANTI-UNION BILL

The Conservative Senators overruled their own speaker in June 2015, an extraordinary step that was unjustified. This was due to Harper pressuring a Bill on unions that was unconstitutional because it violated privacy regulations.

HARPER'S EX-PARLIAMENTARY SECRETARY JAILED FOR BREAKING ELECTION LAW

Stephen Harper's Parliamentary Secretary, who was frequently scapegoated to avoid consequences, was sentenced to jail for his own election spending violations, as reported by the media in June 2015.

CONSERVATIVES BAR CROSBIE CANDIDACY

Ches Crosbie, son of a former Conservative cabinet minister, John Crosbie, was blocked from running for the party in Newfoundland in June 2015. This is an example of how the party, under Harper's leadership, infringed on someone's democratic rights. John Crosby spoke about his son, "You've already been savaged in the back once... You appeal it, you'll get stabbed in the back again. What's the point?" He was displeased with the decision.

CONSERVATIVES ASKED CAMPAIGN EVENT ATTENDEES TO SIGN THE GAG ORDER

Stephen Harper's campaign organizers were advised that his 2015 campaign events should be restricted and that only invitees should be allowed to attend. All invitees were required to sign an agreement not to disclose any information, description, or images about the event. However, this decision was discarded after the media made it a concern.

BILL C-51 AND C-24

Harper conservatives introduced numerous bills in parliament that have paved the way not only for second-class citizenship (Bill C-24) but also for the destruction of the very fabric of Canadian society's diversity and freedom (Bill C-51).

ABUSE OF THE PROCESS WITH OMNIBUS BILLS

Harper's government had accelerated legislation through Parliament by using omnibus bills much more frequently than ever before. This was an abuse of the democratic process. An omnibus bill bypasses many controversial laws and regulations so swiftly that one cannot recognize, review, or reject parts of its content. Former Auditor General Sheila Fraser stated that Canadians rely on Parliament to fulfill its responsibilities, but since Parliament's credibility has been undermined, it has been unable to fulfill the role that Canadians expect of it.

ABUSE OF POWER FOR SILENCING OF THE PUBLIC SERVICE

The PMO has designed a system that allows the Harper Conservative government to exert control over the bureaucracy, following an internal Privy Council staff member's suggestion that the Council had become heavily influenced by the government. The role of the public service in policy work had drastically decreased, leading the Council to become politicized.

LOYALTY OATHS FOR PUBLIC SERVANTS

Archivists and librarians were forced to take strict oaths of allegiance, and their freedom of speech and expression was infringed as restrictions were imposed on them. Academics from both the right and the left wing described this as disturbing.

CONSERVATIVES STOP ACCREDITATION FOR OPPOSITION MPS

In another example of Harper Conservatives adopting hyper-partisan behaviour, the Harper government prevented opposition members from being recognized at international environmental conferences and from visiting military bases.

USING PUBLIC SERVANTS TO FALSELY PRESENT AS CITIZENS IN A STAGED CITIZENSHIP RENEWAL

Some public servants were used as puppets who falsely presented themselves as citizens in a staged Citizenship Renewal that was organized by the Immigration Department. Media outlets compared this event to the practices undertaken by North Korean dictators.

RESTRICTING THE FREEDOM OF SPEECH OF DIPLOMATS

Diplomats were required to have approval of their correspondence from the Conservative political centre, and the country's ambassadors were hardly heard. Commenting on this, a former UN ambassador said our political culture under the Harper conservatives descended into "a nadir of indignity."

RECORD USE OF PERSONAL ATTACK ADS

The Tories, under Stephen Harper's leadership, regularly started airing personal attack ads outside of election times. They were one of the governments that aired the most political attack ads and used controversial content.

SENATE APPOINTMENTS

Harper appointed many Conservative loyalists to the Senate, and several of them were suspended for allegations of financial misconduct. It was revealed that his own chief of staff was involved in some of these issues. One of his Conservative senators quit the Conservative caucus after allegations of a sexual relationship with a teenager.

ECONOMIC ACTION PLAN

The Harper Conservative Government's Economic Action Plan was reported to benefit only the richest 1% of Canadians, increasing the divide between rich and poor.

REFUSING TO SIGN THE UN DECLARATION OF CLEAN WATER AS A HUMAN RIGHT

Indigenous peoples of Canada have limited access to clean water. The Harper Conservative government refused to sign the UN Declaration in September 2007, which recognized clean water as a Human Right of Indigenous peoples.

DAMAGING CANADA'S INTERNATIONAL REPUTATION

The Harper government destroyed Canada's international reputation as a peacekeeping nation when it was made public that Afghan detainees were handed over to the Afghan authorities, most likely to be tortured.

PICKING AND CHOOSING REFUGEES BASED ON THEIR RELIGION

Stephen Harper committed to only admitting 10,000 Iraqi and Syrian refugees. Harper said, while he was responding to questions, that he wants to "make sure that we are selecting the most vulnerable bona fide refugees ... with a focus on the religious and ethnic minorities that are the most vulnerable." The Conservatives had posted an image that read "supporting religious minorities" with a video of Harper delivering this message standing in a Coptic church. The decision to pick and choose the "religious minorities" as reported by the media in 2015 was due to a bias of the government against Muslims, and Harper Conservatives were also violating United Nations principles governing refugee resettlement.

PASSING A BILL GIVING ITSELF THE POWER TO COVER UP ITS OWN CRIMES

In May 2015, Suzanne Legault, an Officer of Parliament, discussed the power grabs undertaken by the Conservative government to cover up a crime committed by the RCMP. The new bill passed by the government was established as a tactic to discharge the RCMP from any of their wrongdoings, following their intentional activity of destroying long-gun registry data. Legault pushed for charges against the RCMP for illegally destroying a record protected by the Access to Information Act. This new bill ended investigations into the RCMP, a power that can be exercised wrongfully.

HARPER GOVERNMENT PARTNERS WITH A FIRM UNDER INVESTIGATION BY THE CRA FOR AN OFFSHORE TAX SCHEME

Stephen Harper hired a major Canadian accounting firm to serve as the formal advisor to CRA, as reported in the media in October 2015, at the same time that CRA was in a legal battle with the accounting firm to crack down on multimillionaires who might have hoarded money offshore.

MINISTER NOT STANDING UP FOR MISSING AND MURDERED INDIGENOUS WOMEN

At the release of the Truth and Reconciliation Commission's report in June 2015, Murray Sinclair called for an investigation regarding the missing and murdered Indigenous women in Canada. As the rest of the room applauded and stood, Bernard Valcourt, Minister of Aboriginal Affairs, did not participate in the standing ovation and remained seated for some time before standing to join the others in solidarity.

NATURAL RESOURCES MINISTER BILLED TAXPAYERS

Natural Resources Minister Greg Rickford spent taxpayer money in July 2015 to attend a fundraiser in Rosedale as a "special guest". The entry ticket was $200 per person. The Stock Exchange event itself on the same day was a $2,700 taxpayer funded event to "deliver remarks and attend meetings." This raised questions about mixing public and party business, including Jason Kenney, Pierre Poilievre, and several other ministers.

CONSERVATIVE WEBSITE PROMOTED TAXPAYER-FUNDED "24/7" VIDEOS

The Conservative Party of Canada promoted Harper on its official website in 2015 through videos produced by 24/7. These vanity videos were funded by taxpayers, and the Conservative Party used them at taxpayers' expense to further promote itself. Stephen Harper contradicted his own statement, saying the money for this election should not be coming from government sources or taxpayers, but rather from the party itself.

Produced by the Privy Council Office, the project would be staffed by taxpayers.

MINISTER WEARS PARTISAN GOLF SHIRT TO TAXPAYER-FUNDED ANNOUNCEMENT

Pierre Poilievre, Employment Minister, attended a Government of Canada event in 2015 to announce the "Universal Childcare Benefit." His appearance sparked controversy, as he wore a polo shirt with the Conservative Party of Canada logo visible while speaking at a taxpayer-funded event. Several Conservative candidates also attended this event, which was held in the children's section of a dollar store located in Ottawa. Canadians found his attire inappropriate, as the event now seemed like a campaigning opportunity for the Conservative Party on public dollars rather than a Government of Canada event.

MINISTER MAKES TAXPAYER-FUNDED ANNOUNCEMENT

To bring awareness to the Universal Childcare Benefit, Employment Minister Poilievre, along with at least four other Conservative candidates, attended a Government of Canada event in July 2015 in the children's section of a Giant Tiger store. Elected officials attended, including Conservative MP Royal Galipeau of Ottawa-Orleans and Abdul Abdi, who won his campaign in Ottawa West-Nepean. However, an unelected

Conservative candidate, Damian Konstantinakos, had also attended the event.

TAXPAYERS POSSIBLY FUNDED WESTERN DIVERSIFICATION MINISTER'S TRIP

Canada's Minister for Western Diversification, Michelle Rempel, was spotted in 2015 mixing government business at a Conservative Party wine tasting fundraiser. Arriving in Edmonton, Rempel was raising funds for Garnett Genius, a Conservative candidate who had not yet been elected. Rempel had even tweeted a promotional photo of a flyer advertising her government event fundraiser, organized by her and Garnet Genius. While taxpayers are uncertain whether her expenses for the fundraiser were paid with public funds, the trip cost taxpayers almost $2,700.

DEPUTY SPEAKER BILLS TAXPAYERS FOR HYPER-PARTISAN MAIL-OUTS

Thousands of taxpayers' dollars were spent mailing promotional flyers to 60,000 homes in MP Barry Devolin's riding of Haliburton-Kawartha Lakes-Brock to promote the plan of the Conservative Party, as reported by the media in June 2015. The public had funded the mailings despite the Board of International Economy stating that doing so was against the rules if it benefited a political party. Many residents who received the mail discovered from the Devolin Office that the public had funded the advertisement distributed by the

Conservative Party. The advertisement promoted the benefits of the Conservative Party while presenting inaccurate information about its opposing parties.

1 BILLION DOLLARS IN PORK BARREL PROJECTS ON THE EVE OF THE 2015 ELECTION

In the 2015 federal elections, the Conservative Party orchestrated several pork barrel projects. Conservative MPs were seen in their ridings in the final days before the election, funding smaller projects in their communities. Government spending in local communities is a tactic parties use to get noticed and win the locals' affections. Conservative MPs had spent the last few days before the election on federal funding, amounting to over $1 billion.

CRA AUDITING GOVERNMENT CRITICS WHILE RIGHT-WING GROUPS APPEAR TO DODGE RULES FOR REPORTING POLITICAL ACTIVITIES

Right-wing charities in Canada are claiming to have conducted zero political activity to the Canada Revenue Agency. Canadian charities are permitted to devote up to 10% of their resources to political activities, but right-wing charities have claimed to have reported 0%. The Fraser Institute and the Atlantic Institute for Market Studies are two right-wing charities that have practiced activities that meet the definition of "political." However, these charities still manage to avoid CRA audits and end up with 0% political activity.

PROPOSING TO CREATE A "BARBARIC CULTURAL PRACTICES" HOTLINE

The Conservative Party decided to establish a police hotline in 2015 to report "barbaric cultural practices." This practice was claimed to further establish Canadian values, which evidently improved their election campaign. However, this ideology of preserving "Canadian values" harmonized with the increase in anti-Muslim hate crimes. The Conservative Party wished to cancel citizenship for convicted terrorists and report "barbaric cultural practices," which puts all Muslims in Canada under scrutiny of the police. The approach the Conservatives took on a minority community within Canada had increased criticism from opposing parties, as their approach may be dangerous to the Muslim community.

CONSERVATIVE MP ALLEGEDLY BUYING ALCOHOL FOR UNDERAGED GIRLS

A Conservative MP was seen photographed drinking with underage girls at a nightclub in 2015. Girls present with this MP tweeted on Twitter regarding the event, publicly announcing their underage drinking provided to them by the MP himself. Shortly after, a friend and supporter of this MP reached out to one of the girls who had tweeted regarding the night and offered her a lifetime VIP membership at the nightclub where the event took place in exchange for taking down the tweets.

BLAMING INDIGENOUS WOMEN FOR THEIR DISAPPEARANCES AND MURDERS

Conservative Party candidates running for office in Prince George-Peace River-Northern Rockies held a debate in October 2015. When the issue of missing and murdered Indigenous women was presented, Conservative candidate Bob Zimmer claimed that one reason for these crimes could be the lack of their employment. NDP opponent Kathi Dickie argued that approximately 1,200 Indigenous women have gone missing or have been murdered between 1980 and 2012 in Canada, and the reason cannot be because of "a lack of a job." Former Prime Minister Harper refused to lead an inquiry regarding the missing and murdered Indigenous women in Canada.

NEGOTIATING A MASSIVE TRADE DEAL IN SECRET AND NOT RELEASING THE DETAILS UNTIL AFTER THE ELECTION

Two weeks prior to the 2015 federal elections, the Government of Canada announced its free-trade agreement, the Trans-Pacific Partnership. As Prime Minister Stephen Harper announced it to the public, only the main highlights and benefits regarding the deal were disclosed. Key information embedded in the agreement's details was not publicized or discussed, leaving Canadians with limited information about the deal right before election day. Given the limited information, many Canadians felt left out and confused regarding whether there were more disadvantages to the deal than its economic advantages.

CONSERVATIVE CAMPAIGN TEAMS CAUGHT ON VIDEO TEARING DOWN ELECTION SIGNS

In 2015, three volunteers from Conservative candidate Bal Gosal's election campaign team were caught in the riding of Brampton Centre tearing down NDP election signs and putting up candidate Bal Gosal's signs. Their actions were caught on video by a Brampton citizen, who uploaded it to YouTube and exposed the volunteers as identifiable members of the Bal Gosal campaign. Gosal had also confirmed that these men were his volunteers.

CONSERVATIVE MP USING "AIR QUOTES" TO DISMISS "RULE OF LAW" DURING C-51 COMMITTEE HEARINGS

In 2015, at a parliamentary hearing on the government's anti-terrorism bill, Conservative MP Diane Ablonczy was dismissive of an amendment that would prevent Canadian judges from violating the Canadian Charter of Rights and Freedoms. The amendment was presented by the Canadian Bar Society, and MP Ablonczy expressed her disapproval. Caught on video, MP Ablonczy was seen using air quotes around "rule of law" and referring to the Principles of Fundamental Justice in a questionable manner, both of which are important terms mentioned in the Canadian Charter.

IGNORING THE VOICE OF CANADIANS REGARDING BILL C-51

The Anti-Terrorism Act, Bill C-51, was passed by the Conservative government in 2015. Despite objections to the bill from a significant segment of the Canadian population, the Conservative government proceeded with it and offered arguments that were widely questioned. Firstly, Conservative MPs, specifically MP LaVar Payne, blamed the critics for promoting conspiracy theories about the Bill. Secondly, Steven Blaney, Minister of Public Safety, referred to the Holocaust to validate the new powers proposed by Bill C-51.

HARPER SAYS THERE ARE TERRORISTS IN MOSQUES

Harper targeted mosques as a source of terrorism in February 2015 while answering a question about the Canadian government's new anti-terrorism legislation. When asked how to distinguish between teens messing around in their basements and someone who is radicalized, he said, "It doesn't matter what the age of the person is, or whether they're in a basement, or whether they're in a mosque or somewhere else."

DEMOTION OF FIRST NATIONS

Harper's Conservative government has been criticized in the media for policies that have threatened the livelihoods of many First Nations' communities. For example, in 2008, Harper decided to discontinue the Kelowna Accord and the five-billion-dollar budget aimed at addressing the socio-economic gap between First Nations and other Canadians. That same year, his government slashed funding for Indigenous languages. In 2009, he declared that Canada had "no history of colonialism," despite evidence suggesting otherwise, including numerous times that Indigenous children died in residential schools. Furthermore, in 2010, the federal government cut funding for the Native Women's Association of Canada (NWAC), which reported that at least six hundred Indigenous women and girls had been murdered or gone missing.

In 2012, the Pickton Inquiry found that the RCMP were misusing their power, as a Human Rights Watch report provided evidence of Indigenous women and girls being assaulted and raped by the Mounties. Harper's government never interfered in this matter, despite the RCMP investigating and finding these allegations to be correct. There was a national outcry for Harper to further inquire into this matter. Instead, he stated, "We should not view this as a sociological phenomenon. We should view it as a crime." Later, he stated that this national inquiry was not a top priority for the federal government. While Harper had served in office as Prime Minister, he and his government had repeatedly denied Indigenous rights and treated themselves as the first people of this land.

This demonstrates the improper use of power Harper exhibited, as Prime Minister, as he provided false information to berate First Nation leaders in the media. This has led many to suggest that Harper has put "social peace" under the radar. The Idle No More movement, which represents the largest and most organized social protest movement in Canada, developed during Harper's tenure as Prime Minister. An individual from the First Nations in Canada lives 7 to 20 years less than the average Canadian, while over half of First Nations' children live in poverty. Indigenous children make up less than 4% of the population, but nearly 50% of all children in foster care nationally. In Manitoba, Indigenous children make up 90% of all children in foster care.

The Harper government had denied providing adequate assistance to address many of the issues First Nations have been encountering. The auditor general reported that First Nations' children are the highest population of children in foster care, suffering a huge gap in education, and the First Nations' housing crisis is worsening. In 2011, the auditor general called out the government's failure to address many of these challenges, which have been threatening the well-being and livelihoods of First Nations communities.

Furthermore, the Office of the Correctional Investigator (OCI) in the past decade declared that their prisons have gotten overpopulated with Indigenous peoples due to Canada's racist and discriminatory policies of the legal and judicial system. The OCI urged the Harper government to act before the situation became worse by following and implementing the OCI's recommendation.

Harper's government made conditions on reserves unlivable. This could have prevented unnecessary deaths from happening and saved many Indigenous peoples from becoming homeless. They have given up their land and natural resources for the Crown to gain and profit to feed the capitalist and economic society. This has come at the expense of sacrificing innocent lives and compromising their well-being. In 2014, the United Nations called on Harper's government for failing to address the poverty in First Nations' communities. This report highlighted the marginalization of First Nations in Canada: their low socio-economic indicators; the crisis of children in foster care; murdered and missing Indigenous women; abusive behaviour by police against Indigenous women, including sexual assaults; and the lack of consultation with First Nations on legislation.

These concerns reflected another report from the same year by the Bertelsmann Foundation, which found that Canada's governance record had declined under Harper's majority government, particularly regarding the First Nations.

USE OF TERRORISTS' PROPAGANDA IN ATTACK AD

Stephen Harper's government created a political ad that misinformed Canadians and was designed to create more fear-mongering regarding the Muslim Community and Islam by associating it with terrorism. They used horrific images and videos of captives from ISIS to promote the ad. The Conservative government did this to attack the Liberal Party leader, Justin Trudeau.

RHETORIC AGAINST MINORITIES AND ISLAMOPHOBIA

Minority groups and the Indigenous peoples of Canada felt disadvantaged under the Harper Conservative government. Muslim and Sikh communities felt targeted under the commands of the Conservative government. Stephen Harper made multiple statements that targeted the Muslim Community in Canada, declaring Islamism as a threat to Canada. In August of 2015, he made a statement which insinuated that Canada was in danger because of a "Violent Global Jihadist Movement." Shortly after the Boston Attack took place in 2013, Harper stated that the Canadian government would develop new legislation incorporating anti-terrorism laws and investigative powers, like the legislation that had terminated in 2007.

The Muslim community feared that new legislation would put a target on their backs because of the previous legislation, which expired in 2007, placed significant surveillance on them after the 9/11 attacks. The Harper government demeaned the Muslim community in Canada, disrupting the peace that Muslim minorities felt in their own communities. When this matter was addressed to the Senate Committee on National Security, the committee failed to invite Canadians, who represented the Muslim Canadian population. Muslims in Canada were afraid to speak up against the conservative government, and that their lives in Canada would have to change because of the misrepresentation of their community.

Canadian minorities feared the power the conservative government was able to exercise over the state. The ideologies presented in Stephen Harper's policies and legislation continued to marginalize Canadian Muslims. These policies created a divide amongst Canadian Muslims and citizens who began to formulate prejudices against the Muslim community, normalizing Islamophobia. Rather than minimizing this divide, the Harper government engaged in this anti-Muslim rhetoric. The government used the term "jihad" frequently as a symbol of its anti-terrorism legislation and went as far as posting false propaganda to mislead Canadians.

Shahina Siddiqui, an award-winning interfaith worker, opposed the Conservative senators in a meeting, pleading for them not to view Muslims as a threat to the country and to steer clear of misleading propaganda that could increase fear. In response, she was told not to be defensive when standing up for the Muslim

Community. She was treated unequally in the meeting with Conservative senators. The Muslim community of Canada were victims of silence as the Harper Conservative government continued to establish a divide and marginalize minorities.

FEDERAL ELECTION 2015

The Harper Conservative government lost its popularity and credibility as its actions began to cause distrust amongst Canadians. Minority groups, First Nations, and many moderate conservatives were disappointed by the Conservative government's misuse of power. In 2015, they suffered a defeat in the federal elections by the Liberal Party under the leadership of Justin Trudeau. The Liberal Party won a majority with 184 seats, compared to 34 in the 2011 election.

CHAPTER 10

Justin Trudeau/Carney Liberals Era (2015-2025)

Justin Pierre James Trudeau was the 23rd prime minister of Canada since 2015 and the leader of the Liberal Party since 2013 up until the 2025 federal election

He was born in Ottawa, Ontario. He acquired a Bachelor of Education degree from the University of British Columbia. After graduating, he taught in a private school in Vancouver before returning to Montreal in 2002. In the 2008 federal election, he was elected to the House of Commons from the riding of Papineau, Montreal. In 2013, Trudeau was elected leader of the Liberal Party, and he led the party to a majority government in the 2015 federal election. He became the second-youngest prime minister in Canadian history after Joe Clark.

During his first term, he established the Canada Child Benefit, legalized medical assistance in dying, legalized recreational marijuana through the Cannabis Act, established the Independent Senate Appointments, and introduced the Federal Carbon Tax. His government negotiated the Canada-United States-Mexico Agreement (CUSMA), the Comprehensive and Progressive Agreement for the Trans-Pacific

Partnership and signed the Paris Agreement on climate change.

In the 2019 election, his Liberal Party was reduced to a minority government. His government faced the challenges of the COVID-19 pandemic. His government announced an "assault-style" weapons ban in response to the 2020 Nova Scotia attacks. Additionally, it launched a national $10-a-day childcare program. He was cleared by the ethics commissioner for his part in the WE Charity scandal. In the 2021 federal election, he led the Liberals to another minority government. In 2022, he invoked the Emergencies Act in response to the Freedom Convoy protests in Ottawa. He imposed sanctions on Russia due to the invasion of Ukraine and authorized military aid to Ukraine. His party signed a confidence-and-supply agreement with the New Democratic Party (NDP) in early 2022, introduced the Canadian Dental Care Plan and national pharmacare in 2024.

Prime Minister Trudeau promised to rebuild relations with Indigenous peoples in Canada. Additionally, he promoted the multicultural policy, emphasizing its acceptance of cultural and ethnic diversity and its welcoming of immigrants. Justin Trudeau has emphasized the importance of multiculturalism as Prime Minister. He acknowledged Canada as a country of respect and unity of all cultures and ethnicities, despite their differences. There has been some opposition towards multiculturalism in Canada from communities in Western Canada and Quebec who are from generations of European colonizers and whose ancestors colonized the land of the Indigenous peoples of Canada.

Racial minorities supported Justin Trudeau in 2015 due to his inclusive policies and the slogan "diversity is our strength." He tried to bridge the divide in society caused by the Conservative government. However, opposition to his government continued to grow in Western Canada, the Conservative Party's base. After winning the second term in 2019 and the third term in 2021, the political division started to grow exponentially. After the sudden resignation of Deputy Prime Minister Chrystia Freeland in December 2024, Trudeau announced on January 6, 2025, that he would resign as both the prime minister and leader of the Liberal Party after the Liberal Party elects a new leader. He prorogued the Parliament until March 24, 2025.

Mark Carney was elected as the new leader of the Liberal Party on March 9th and became the 24th Prime Minister of Canada.

Public Records

JUSTIN TRUDEAU MARCHED IN THE PRIDE PARADES – CONTROVERSY STARTS

Justin Trudeau became the first Prime Minister to attend Pride parades in 2016. At a pride parade in Halifax, he wore a pink shirt and white pants and marched alongside his wife. He waved "Happy Pride!" to people along the parade route. This created a division in public opinion, with disapproval among conservative and faith-based communities.

VACATION ON AGA KHAN ISLAND - VIOLATION OF CONFLICT OF INTEREST

During Christmas break in 2016, Justin Trudeau and his family vacationed on Aga Khan Island, a private island owned by a billionaire who was a close friend of the family. This decision by the prime minister sparked backlash, as the ethics commissioner launched investigations following the Conservative Party's contact about Trudeau's visit.

Trudeau believed he had not committed any ethical violation because the private island was owned by a close family friend, whom he considered an exception. Though earlier that year, the Aga Khan Foundation Canada received funding from the federal government. After the investigation, it was found that he violated the conflict-of-interest code. He was the first Prime Minister to have violated the Conflict-of-Interest Act for a vacation to Aga Khan's private island.

Although evidence showed that no business was discussed during the vacation and that it was purely for enjoyment, it was considered unethical to accept a gift of property use from friends who participate in business affairs with the Canadian government.

QUEBEC CITY MOSQUE SHOOTING

On January 29th, 2017, a 27-year-old man, Alexandre Bissonnette, murdered six people and injured many in an attack in the Quebec City Mosque. He had then turned himself in to the police after fleeing the scene. In March of 2018, Bissonnette had pleaded guilty to 6 first-degree murder charges and six accounts of attempted murder after a series of evidence was presented in court. The evidence against Bissonnette portrayed him as a right-wing figure who praised white nationalist leaders. This crime was motivated by hatred towards the Muslim community. It was ruled as a hate crime because of the fear of Muslims and minorities that was promoted by the right-wing campaign. Bissonnette had, in fact, told the police that he feared Muslims.

This hate crime brought more awareness to the Islamophobic crimes against Muslims. In the year of the shooting, there were 349 reported hate crimes against Muslims in Canada alone. Islamophobic hate crimes go against Canada's multicultural policy and violate the rights and freedoms of minorities mentioned in the Charter. Islamophobia was at its peak during Harper's Conservative government, whereas Justin Trudeau called these victims a group of innocent people targeted for practicing their faith, calling this attack a terrorist act. Although retracted later upon the public uproar, Francois Legault, the premier of Quebec, denied the existence of Islamophobia in Quebec after attending a memorial for the victims. This deepened the divide between minorities and the Quebec government.

CONSERVATIVE SENATOR LYNN BEYAK DEFENDS RESIDENTIAL SCHOOLS

In March 2017, Conservative Senator Lynn Beyak criticized the findings of the Truth and Reconciliation Commission that the residential school system, founded by Prime Minister John A Macdonald, caused physical, mental, and sexual abuse of Indigenous children and resulted in the deaths of at least six thousand children from malnutrition and disease. The bodies of many of these children were never returned to their parents. Senator Beyak said that those findings overshadowed the "good deeds" of "well-intentioned" residential school workers.

CANCELLATION OF THE ENERGY EAST PIPELINE

The Energy East Pipeline was a proposed pipeline running from Alberta east to Saint John, New Brunswick. If it were built, it would be the largest oil pipeline in North America, running the full length of New Brunswick. To accommodate the pipeline, new pump stations and tank facilities would be constructed. The 16-billion-dollar pipeline proposal was announced in August 2013. The proposal was pursued as TransCanada Pipelines filed its application to the National Energy Board in 2014. In 2017, this pipeline proposal was cancelled. TransCanada's decision to cancel the pipeline disappointed the oil industry and devastated many people in Alberta. The cancellation of the Energy East pipeline further widened the divide between Eastern and Western Canada.

CONSERVATIVE PARTY LEADERSHIP ELECTION 2017

Andrew Scheer was elected the leader of the Conservative Party on the thirteenth ballot, narrowly defeating Maxime Bernier. Conservative politicians support the right-wing ideology. In May 2017, one of the Conservative Party's leadership candidates, Kellie Leitch, referred to Trump's victory in 2016 as an "exciting message and one that we need delivered in Canada as well." She suggested the screening of new immigrants for "anti-Canadian" values, which many thought was equal to Trump's immigration restrictions. Although another leadership candidate, who withdrew mid-race, said his policies were different from Trump's, he was compared to Trump in the media.

CONTROVERSY OF THE LEGALIZATION OF RECREATIONAL MARIJUANA

Justin Trudeau started advocating for the legalization of marijuana in 2013 while speaking at a rally in Kelowna, B.C. He said that imposing a tax on its sale and regulating it were the only ways to keep it out of the hands of youth. He admitted to using Marijuana in 2010 when he was a Member of Parliament. He reiterated his support for legalization in Canada and stated that

Canada would benefit from the experiences of Colorado and <u>Washington</u>.

The Liberal government introduced Bill C-45, the Cannabis Act, which was passed in November 2017. In October 2018, cannabis became legal in Canada for both recreational and medicinal use. This raised significant concern among the public, healthcare professionals and law enforcement agencies. It may not be as big a source of revenue for the government as it was initially interpreted to be. The black market might continue selling it because of the price difference and because it can be sold to those who cannot get it due to the age limit. The relation of cannabis use with psychiatric conditions, traffic accidents, crimes, harmful effects on the fetus, and increased use by the public after legalization have been the major concerns. Additionally, its harmful effects may not become apparent until later in life.

A controversy started about the impact of recreational Cannabis on the health of Canadians. Some argued that legalizing recreational marijuana is not only economically beneficial for the country but also saves lives. Those who supported legalizing recreational marijuana said that it reduces opioid abuse and overdose deaths.

Those who were against the legislation of the recreational use of cannabis cited that in Washington state, the number of traffic accidents due to marijuana impaired drivers doubled in the years after its legalization. In Colorado, since the legalization of recreational marijuana in 2012, fatal accidents involving marijuana have increased by 62%. In Colorado, marijuana-related hospitalization increased by an average of 30% every year since its legalization, and marijuana-related poisoning increased exponentially in both Colorado and Washington states. Physicians in the Children's Hospital in Denver, USA, reported that after the legalization of recreational marijuana, the emergency department was treating 1 to 2 children per month for accidental ingestion of marijuana.

When Colorado legalized marijuana, it became the number one state in the US for the highest use of marijuana, with rates of more than 12 percent. The black market for drugs in both Washington and Colorado had also exploded with crime groups since the legalization of marijuana.

It goes unnoticed how marijuana can harm non-smokers due to secondhand use. Marijuana edibles, which include candy and cookies, increase the risk for children, in addition to pets. Furthermore, the advertisements for marijuana edibles will become common like soft drinks, making it more accessible to the public. Studies have linked the consumption of marijuana with mental health illnesses such as anxiety and bipolar disorders.

Marijuana is also responsible for relationship issues, poor academic performance, employment issues, and impaired cognitive function, including memory issues and lower intelligence quotient. The consequences of the legalization of marijuana will unfold over time. Evidence shows that the human brain continues to mature until age 25. The use of marijuana by young consumers will have dangerous effects on the developing brain.

JAGMEET SINGH BECAME THE LEADER OF THE NDP

On October 1, 2017, Jagmeet Singh, a Toronto MPP, became the leader of the Federal NDP. He won the leadership vote on the first ballot. He was later elected as an MP in a by-election from B.C.

ONLINE THREATS AGAINST JUSTIN TRUDEAU

Several people were found making threats against Prime Minister Justin Trudeau, his family, and minorities. A thirty-four-year-old man from Saskatchewan was arrested in 2017 for threatening Prime Minister Justin Trudeau and posting on Facebook that the Prime Minister should be shot. Another woman in southern Alberta made online threats against the Prime Minister's wife, Sophie Grégoire Trudeau. A Quebec man was also charged with making online threats against Prime Minister Justin Trudeau and the Muslim community in Longueuil, Quebec.

CONTROVERSY OF LIBERALS' SEX EDUCATION CURRICULUM IN ONTARIO

In 2015, Kathleen Wynne, the premier of Ontario, introduced a new sex education curriculum with many changes since 1998, which included explicit content, sexual orientation, and gender identity. Wynne was the first woman and the first openly gay person to serve as Premier of Ontario. This led to many protests across Ontario against the new curriculum, which drew strongly polarized reactions. Many thought it was inappropriate and against parents' rights, while supporters argued that it was necessary to help vulnerable minorities. The conservative and faith-based communities argued that it introduced "too much, too soon," and many parents said that they would pull their children out of public schools. They also argued that the government had not sufficiently consulted parents.

In April 2015, a large demonstration against this new curriculum was held at Queen's Park in Toronto. During the 2018 Progressive Conservative Party of Ontario leadership election, many candidates led attacks against the 2015 curriculum changes. Winner of the leadership race, Doug Ford, argued that parents should have the final say on education. The Ontario Liberal Party lost very badly in the 2018 election, with Wynn conceding before the election.

GROPING ALLEGATIONS

In 2018, a media report stated that in 2000, Trudeau attended a charity fundraising event in Creston, B.C. At this event, he was accused of groping a female reporter. The female reporter said the incident occurred, but Trudeau apologized the next day. She did not pursue the incident and said she had no contact with Trudeau before or after he became prime minister. Trudeau apologized and said he was confident he had not acted inappropriately, but that people can experience interactions differently.

HARPER PRAISED TRUMP ON PULLING OUT OF THE IRAN NUCLEAR DEAL.

In May 2018, The New York Times published an article about Trump's decision to withdraw from the Iran Nuclear Deal. Several prominent political figures expressed serious concerns about Trump's decision, but the former prime minister Stephen Harper was very pleased with the call to withdraw from the Joint Comprehensive Plan of Action (JCPOA) on Iran. Former American President Obama expressed concern over this decision, saying it was "misguided" and would only hurt the credibility of the US on the international stage. Obama praised the deal, calling it a success in diplomacy, and also said that it has prevented Iran from developing its nuclear program. Many other world leaders had promised to continue honouring the deal.

Prime Minister Justin Trudeau expressed his regret over the US pulling out of the agreement.

CONSERVATIVE MP MAXIME BERNIER LAUNCHES THE PEOPLE'S PARTY

Maxime Bernier, Conservative MP, declared the Conservative Party morally and financially corrupt and launched a new political party, the People's Party of Canada, on September 14, 2018. Bernier was a former Conservative Minister who lost the leadership contest a year ago. Bernier has always defended his views by claiming they reflect genuine conservative ideas. The People's Party of Canada is considered a right-wing political party and supports the notion of "ending official multiculturalism," ending "glorification of diversity," and denies that climate change exists. He promised to fight any motion in Parliament that contained the word "Islamophobia." Bernier has opposed Canada's immigration policy and highlighted the "Migrant Crisis" as one of the major issues that political parties are not paying enough attention to.

NDP Leader Jagmeet Singh had addressed Maxime Bernier for spreading hatred and division and inciting fear. Singh also objected to Bernier's invitation to debate, expressing his disapproval of many of Bernier's ideas. Bernier attended a rally with the neo-Nazi group, Soldiers of Odin. The party's former leader engaged in Islamophobic rhetoric, such as calling Islam "pure evil," and argued it was time to speak about Muslim's acceptance in Canada. One candidate threatened a mosque for wanting to sue them, as he was not invited to a community town hall. The National Council of Canadian Muslims (NCCM) was apprehensive of Maxime Bernier using the 2019 federal elections as an opportunity to incite fear, hate, and division. Bernier lost his position as MP in his home riding of Beauce, Quebec. His riding is not too far from Quebec City, where Alexandre Bissonnette opened fire and killed six Muslim congregants and injured many on January 29, 2017, at a mosque in Quebec City. The same mosque had received several online threats and a pig's head that was left by someone unidentified. Additionally, the executive members of this mosque became targets of an arson attack. Maxime Bernier did not condemn this attack.

Maxime Bernier never condemned the Christchurch attack that occurred in New Zealand. He introduced his party's platform, speaking out against multiculturalism. He was seen standing with a keynote speaker at a party conference, accusing Liberals of "infesting" their party with Muslims candidates. This same individual was at Maxime Bernier's inaugural party in August of 2020.

In 2021, Mr. Bernier launched a nationwide tour opposing pandemic lockdowns and mandatory vaccinations. Although his statements were perceived as opposed to the public health measures, many people joined his rallies. He was issued tickets and arrested for breaking public health rules. In the 2021 election, although his party did not secure any seats, his popular vote increased significantly from the 2019 election.

TRUDEAU'S 2018 INDIA VISIT CONTROVERSY

When Justin Trudeau visited India in 2018, a supporter of the Khalistan movement and Sikh separatist, Jaspal Atwal, was invited and photographed with Trudeau at an event in Mumbai. Jaspal Atwal was found guilty of the attempted murder of an Indian politician and was sentenced to 20 years in prison. Justin Trudeau's visit to India raised significant criticism.

CANADA ARRESTED MENG WANZHOU

In December 2018, Canada arrested Meng Wanzhou, the CFO of the Chinese telecom giant Huawei and the daughter of its founder, at Vancouver airport on a U.S. warrant for violating sanctions against Iran. This caused diplomatic tension between China and Canada, and China decided to detain two Canadians—Michael Kovrig and Michael Spavor on national security charges. When Meng was released under a deferred prosecution agreement with the U.S. Department of Justice, China also released both detained Canadians.

SNC LAVALIN SCANDAL

In 2011, the investigation into SNC-Lavalin began following allegations that millions of dollars had been paid to Libyan government officials as bribes. In 2018, Prime Minister Trudeau established the option of a Deferred Prosecution Agreement (DPA) under the Criminal Code. SNC Lavalin had approached the Director of Public Prosecution for a DPA but was denied their request. Minister of Justice and Attorney General Jody Wilson-Raybould had the authority to overrule this decision. In February 2019, after Jody Wilson-Raybould was appointed Minister of Veterans Affairs, she came forward to say that Prime Minister Trudeau allegedly pressured her to grant SNC-Lavalin a DPA.

After the investigation into Prime Minister Trudeau, the ethics commissioner concluded that Trudeau had taken advantage of his authority to pressure the Attorney General to grant approval for the SNC-Lavalin DPA, thereby breaching ethics. This significantly impacted Liberal popularity in the October 2019 election. Jody Wilson-Raybould ran as an independent candidate and was elected.

"UNITED WE ROLL" CONVOY TO OTTAWA AND YELLOW VEST GROUP

In February 2019, many people from Western Canada participated in the United We Roll convoy to Ottawa. They said they were there to unite Canadians around a pipeline issue and have the Liberal government cancel bills C-69 and C-48. There were many right-wing groups with signs denouncing the global migration pact and accusing Justin Trudeau of treason. Many convoy participants wore hats that said, "Make Canada Great Again," similar to US President Donald Trump's slogan. This convoy had support from high-profile Conservative politicians, including Conservative Party leader Andrew Scheer, who addressed the group.

A Conservative senator told the crowd to "roll over" Liberals across the country, and he refused to apologize. The rally was associated with Yellow Vests Canada, a group with anti-immigrant views. The members of the Yellow Vests Facebook group have advocated for MP Iqra Khalid to be deported, called visible minorities sub-human and scum, and made death threats against Justin Trudeau.

Harper's Conservative government's decision to ban the niqab in citizenship ceremonies and implement a tip line for "barbaric cultural practices" had already disappointed minorities. Failure to acknowledge and condemn these slogans sent a message that the party was aligned with the right-wing extremists. Scheer could have spoken at the United We Roll rally and supported the oil and gas industry while simultaneously condemning racism, but instead, he clearly said, "We're standing with you." He should have shown political courage like in the US presidential election in 2008, Republican John McCain defended Barack Obama against racist questions from participants in a town hall. The Conservatives' failure to draw a line between grievances about the oil and gas industry and illegitimate grievances about immigrants and minorities escalated the division among voters.

CONSERVATIVE MP MICHAEL COOPER READS THE MANIFESTO OF THE NEW ZEALAND TERRORIST

In May 2019, Conservative MP Mr. Cooper quoted from the manifesto of the man responsible for murdering more than fifty innocent Muslims by carrying out a terrorist attack on a mosque in Christchurch, New Zealand. Reading this manifesto in New Zealand is a criminal activity. It was seen as Mr. Cooper's attempt to discredit the testimony of a Muslim justice committee witness.

RANA ZAMAN WAS REMOVED AS A CANDIDATE FROM NDP

In June 2019, the New Democratic Party (NDP) removed Rana Zaman as their federal candidate for the Dartmouth—Cole Harbour riding in Nova Scotia because of her social media post from 2018 in support of the "Great March of Return" in Gaza. She apologized for her social media post later and joined the Green Party of Canada.

QUEBEC BILL 21 AND JUSTIN TRUDEAU'S INACTION

The Quebec government introduced Bill 21 in June 2019, legislation that restricts religious symbolism in public services. Bill 21 restricts public service employees, such as police officers, teachers, and other professionals, from wearing religious symbols while performing their duties. It was like a legislation in 2017 that banned face coverings for those either receiving or providing public services.

Many citizens in Quebec were against this Bill, declaring that it targets minority religious groups, stopping them from their religious freedom. Although the Quebec Charter of Rights and Freedoms guarantees freedom of religion to all people of the province, the Charter will now include a declaration of state secularism, remaining religiously neutral. After much debate, Bill 21 passed, banning teachers, judges, and other public service professionals from wearing items such as turbans, kippahs, and hijabs while on duty.

Although Quebec has adjusted its Charter to be able to incorporate such a bill in its province, the bill goes against the tolerance that Canada embraces. The bill leads to the mistreatment of minority Quebecers in Quebec.

The Quebec government passed Bill 21 in June 2019, banning public servants from wearing religious symbols. A vast majority of the Canadian population, especially minorities, believed that Justin Trudeau would take the lead in fighting the Quebec government over Bill 21. Unfortunately, he did little more than share a few words on this issue. Although he said Quebec was violating what Canada was known for, federal leaders were criticized for not pursuing the fight further and allowing the bill to pass. Regarding the Quebec government's abuse of power in passing Bill 21, rather than revoking the powers of some of Quebec's special arrangements, the federal government rewarded Premier Francois Legault by granting him the authority to appoint three Quebec justices to the Supreme Court of Canada. Following Bill 21, decisions by both the Quebec provincial and federal governments in Canada divided public opinion across the country.

As a result of this law, a teacher in Quebec was fired in December 2021 for wearing a headscarf, i.e., a hijab. Prime Minister Justin Trudeau was aware of this law and this incident. In fact, journalists have questioned him several times if he would take any practical action against this discriminatory law. He has always given statements that did not reflect any real commitment on his part to end this law.

THE FEDERAL GOVERNMENT INTRODUCED A CARBON TAX

The Canadian federal government introduced a price on carbon in 2019, starting at $20 per ton of carbon dioxide or equivalent. In 2016, Canada announced its endorsement of the Paris Agreement. Canada aimed to reduce Canadian emissions by 40-45% below 2005 levels by 2030 and to reach net-zero by 2050. Erin O'Toole had promised the Conservatives to scrap Trudeau's tax plan and introduce his own plan by implementing a 'personal low-carbon savings' for all Canadians. This would work by paying the same carbon tax on gasoline and home heating that the Liberals initially planned to charge; however, the proceeds go into a savings account in the individual's name. These savings can be used to purchase green-friendly products such as efficient furnaces, bicycles, and bus passes, as well as other rewards that reduce emissions.

The motion at the Conservative Party convention that asked delegates to acknowledge that "Canadian businesses classified as highly polluting need to take more responsibility" and "reduce their GHG emissions" was defeated, with the vote 54 to 46%. This led to a backlash on social media, calling the Conservative Party a party of climate deniers.

BLACK FACE SCANDAL

Shortly after the SNC-Lavalin affair, on September 18th, 2019, during the 2019 election campaign, photos of Justin Trudeau wearing blackface surfaced on the internet. These images were first publicized by Time Magazine, sourced from a yearbook photo dating back to 2001, when Justin Trudeau was a teacher. In the photo, Trudeau dressed as Aladdin with blackface makeup. Prime Minister Trudeau faced backlash for his poor decisions as these images went viral online. As Trudeau fights for diversity and against racism, these pictures made both supporters and non-supporters question these dual standards. Minorities in Canada have always supported Trudeau because of how he prioritized the issue of racism. Many of his supporters were disappointed by these images, and Justin Trudeau's popularity as a leader declined.

FEDERAL ELECTION 2019

The 2019 Canadian federal election was held on October 21, 2019, and the Liberal Party, led by incumbent Prime Minister Justin Trudeau, won, forming a single-party minority government. The Liberals lost the popular vote to the Conservative Party.

The Conservative Party, the official opposition led by Andrew Scheer, won 121 seats. The Bloc Québécois won thirty-two seats, regained official party status, and became the third party for the first time since 2008. The New Democratic Party won twenty-four seats, its worst performance since 2004. The Green Party won three seats. Independent MP Jody Wilson-Raybould also won her seat.

RESIGNATION OF ANDREW SCHEER AFTER THE 2019 ELECTION

The Conservatives lost the 2019 federal election. Andrew Scheer claimed to represent "all Canadians," but minorities were not satisfied with his position. He never acknowledged that Muslims were the ones targeted in the attack that occurred in Christchurch, New Zealand. Additionally, his campaign manager was reported to be a past director of the far-right, Islamophobic Rebel Media.

Andrew Scheer has also advised Canadians not to believe the "narrative" from mainstream media, but to "challenge," and "double check and consult" smart, independent, objective organizations such as *True North.*

After the 2019 election, there was some criticism from the Conservative Party insiders regarding Mr. Scheer's performance in the election campaign and calls for stepping down. Mr. Scheer has repeatedly said that he would not withdraw from party leadership and lead a strong opposition into the next parliament. Former Conservative cabinet minister Peter MacKay criticized Scheer's inability to clearly articulate his position on social issues like abortion and same-sex marriage.

Andrew Scheer was criticized in the media for spreading misinformation during his October 2019 election campaign. When Andrew Scheer was the Speaker, he pointed out a Liberal MP who had been targeted by fake robocalls. Scheer suggested that he had no authority over the matter. It was later revealed that in 2011, when the robocall voter suppression was taking place, Andrew Scheer's riding associate in Saskatchewan, Regina-Qu'Appelle, sent $3,000 to a Conservative Guelph campaign. Opposition MPs blamed Scheer for obstructing debate on the Robocall Scandal, which led to the imprisonment of a Conservative staffer.

The Ethics Watchdog Democracy called on the Commissioner of Canada Elections to launch an investigation into whether the Tories and CAPP broke the Canada Elections Act. The Conservative Party dismissed nearly 1,400 members after several complaints of possible fraud in the registration process. The dispute escalated as Scheer won the leadership contest. Before becoming a politician, Andrew Scheer claimed to be an insurance broker. The Globe and Mail reported that it found no record of Scheer ever having received a license to practice as an insurance broker or agent in Saskatchewan. Andrew Scheer confirmed that he had dual citizenship (Canadian and American) and was in the process of relinquishing his US citizenship, but he never provided proof of its relinquishment. He also denied giving an explanation about how he was able to travel to the US without having a valid American passport.

Scheer accused Justin Trudeau of raising taxes when he was confronted with allegations of a possible Liberal-NDP coalition to increase the GST rate. When the terrorist attack at the Christchurch Mosque occurred in New Zealand, PM Justin Trudeau was quick to condemn and acknowledge that white nationalist inspired terrorism was a growing problem. In contrast, Scheer tweeted that the attack was an attack on "freedom," rather than on Muslim worshippers. It took

Scheer to receive criticism and anger to issue a second statement. Some Conservative MPs also criticized his statement as inappropriate, not condemning it, and not sympathizing enough with those affected by it. The two statements he issued specified what had happened and acknowledged that Muslims were targeted because of their faith. The Conservative Party could not recover in the 2019 elections, and there was division within the party. Although Mr. Scheer had announced that he would continue leading the Conservative Party, in December 2019, he resigned amid allegations of the misuse of party funds.

PANDEMIC OF COVID-19

The Liberal government faced the challenge of COVID-19 soon after winning a minority government in 2019. The pandemic caused significant damage to the Canadian economy and social life. The government followed public health guidelines, but there was criticism of its policies, including delays in border control and in vaccine availability. Justin Trudeau's government implemented several support programs for Canadians and businesses affected by COVID-19. As a result of government overspending, the deficit widened, and inflation rose sharply. There were ongoing controversies and many protests about vaccine passports. During the 2021 election campaign, there were many protests against Trudeau by anti-vaxxers, led by some Canadian politicians.

CANADIAN POLITICIANS BREAKING THE RULES OF THE PANDEMIC

Due to the pandemic, Public Health recommended avoiding nonessential travel, making holiday celebrations difficult. Not only were politicians preaching to citizens not to meet, arrange parties, or visit each other, but police were raiding people's houses, arresting and issuing heavy fines. People were restricted from supporting their dying relatives or visiting their senior parents in long-term care homes. Ironically, many MPs, MPPS, MLAs, senators, and ministers were identified travelling abroad for vacations during the ongoing COVID-19 pandemic, as if they were exempt from these rules. Some issued pre-recorded New Year Season Greetings videos, as if they were in Canada. Conservative MP from Ontario David Sweet, Alberta's Conservative MP Ron Liepert, Conservative Senator Don Plett, NDP MP Niki Ashton, Liberal MPs Kamal Khera, Sameer Zuberi, Alexandra Mendès, Quebec Liberal MNA Pierre Arcand, several MLAs in Alberta, and Ontario MPP and Minister Rod Phillips left the country during the pandemic against the public health rules. These were some of the MPs who breached the restrictions enforced on the Canadian population. Indeed, Senator Plett's last question in the Senate before the holiday break implied that Trudeau was granted special treatment from the rules enforced in the fight against the pandemic, as he was seen visiting the Ottawa hospital where COVID-19 vaccines were being administered, despite pandemic restrictions on visitors.

ALBERTA MINISTER OF HEALTH SHOWING UP TO THREATEN A CALGARY PHYSICIAN AT HIS HOUSE

In March 2020, Tylor Shandro, the minister of health for Alberta, showed up at the driveway of Calgary family physician Dr. Mukarram Zaidi with his wife at about 7 p.m. on Saturday, when Dr. Zaidi's two teenage sons were playing basketball in their driveway. According to Dr. Zaidi, Shandro told his sons that he wanted to speak to Dr. Zaidi and they should stay inside," because "they didn't want to listen to what was going to happen. Shandro was threatening and yelling at Dr. Zaidi. Dr. Zaidi has raised his concerns about the Alberta government's changes to healthcare policy. There were many calls for Shandro's resignation across Alberta.

MP DEREK SLOAN QUESTIONED THE LOYALTY OF CANADA'S CHIEF PUBLIC HEALTH OFFICER

Conservative MP Derek Sloan questioned the loyalty of Canada's Chief Public Health Officer in April 2020, accusing her of working for China. Derek Sloan's statements were widely criticized in the media.

WE CHARITY SCANDAL

In the summer of 2020, Justin Trudeau announced a program that would financially support students. The federal government announced that it had chosen the

WE Charity to manage a $912 million-dollar student grant program.

Since the WE Charity had ties to the Trudeau Family, the opposition parties had filed various complaints with the ethics commissioner regarding a conflict of interest. These complaints led to further investigations in which Trudeau was accused of using his relationship with the WE Charity. Because of these complaints, the federal government and WE Charity decided to part ways, with the federal government taking control of the grant.

Due to this issue, there was a delay in students' opportunities to volunteer and receive grants, which deeply impacted those in need of support during the COVID-19 pandemic. This led to a decline in polling for the Liberal Party and a drop in Justin Trudeau's popularity. The scandal has also damaged the WE Charity's reputation.

RESIGNATION OF FINANCE MINISTER BILL MORNEAU

In August of 2020, Finance Minister Bill Morneau resigned due to his ties to the WE Charity and reports of disagreement with Justin Trudeau over how much funding was needed to recover from the pandemic.

ATTACK ON THE PRIME MINISTER'S RESIDENCE IN OTTAWA

Corey Hurren, a 46-year-old sausage-maker from Manitoba who served with the military, rammed a gate at Rideau Hall before heading towards Prime Minister Justin Trudeau's home in July 2020. Police were able to arrest him. He was initially accused of making threats of death or bodily harm to Trudeau. He said he wanted to arrest Trudeau because of implementing COVID-19 restrictions and a ban on assault-style firearms. He believed that Trudeau was turning Canada into a communist state. He was found to have exchanges with friends about conspiracy theories that COVID-19 was a hoax.

ERIN O'TOOLE WAS ELECTED AS THE NEW LEADER OF THE CONSERVATIVE PARTY

Erin O'Toole was elected the leader of the Conservative Party in August 2020. He took 57 percent of the votes on the third ballot, compared to 43 percent for Peter MacKay. O'Toole took support from Leslyn Lewis, who dropped off after the second ballot. Derek Sloan dropped off after the first ballot.

ERIN O'TOOLE – INTRODUCING CHANGES IN THE IMAGE OF THE CONSERVATIVE PARTY

Since Erin O'Toole was elected the new leader of the Conservative Party, he has been trying to change the Party's historical image. While he was trying to eliminate the anti-minority rhetoric built by Harper Conservatives, his own deputy leader was found to be wearing a MAGA hat. Mr. O'Toole has promoted a slogan of "take back Canada" in his leadership campaign. In October 2020, a Léger poll for 338 Canada found that the number of "pro-Trump conservatives" in the Conservative Party of Canada had significantly increased. Maclean's suggested that this might explain O'Toole's "True Blue" campaign, with slogans like "Take Back Canada," a Canadian version of Trump's slogan "Make America Great Again," as part of his leadership campaign. In a video, O'Toole called upon Canadians to "join our fight, let's take back Canada."

In a CBC interview in September 2020, when asked where his "Canada First" policy differed from Trump's "America First" policy, O'Toole said, "No, it was not."

The Conservative Party website had slogans like "Trudeau is rigging the election," which was similar to what Mr. Trump has said after his defeat in the 2020 election. Although Mr. O'Toole said that he stopped appearing on the show because of its divisive approach, his interview with Rebel Media still created controversy.

ERIN O'TOOLE'S STATEMENT REGARDING RESIDENTIAL SCHOOLS

The deep-rooted mistreatment of the Indigenous peoples by the Canadian government has left a significant scar on Canadian history, still affecting Indigenous peoples today. A nationwide issue regarding residential schools has been ongoing with the discovery of unmarked graves of the Indigenous children who suffered physical and sexual abuse and died in residential schools. Many Canadians have been debating and fighting for changes to the names and statues of leaders who founded institutions such as residential schools. Being the talk of the town, Ryerson University had many debates about whether they should tear down Egerton Ryerson's name and his statue. Egerton Ryerson was a methodologist and educator who established the public education system in Ontario. However, Egerton Ryerson was also the founder of the residential school system.

During a Zoom discussion with students at TMU about residential schools, O'Toole said, "When Egerton Ryerson was called in by Hector Langevin and people, it was meant to try and provide education." These comments caused nationwide whiplash over O'Toole's lack of knowledge about residential schools. Erin O'Toole also discussed the Liberal Party's involvement in opening several residential schools and mentioned former Prime Minister Jean Chrétien for opening three. Jean Chrétien was not the prime minister when a single residential school opened; instead, he was the prime minister when eleven residential schools were closed. At least sixty-seven residential schools were also closed off the 159 listed while Pierre Trudeau was Prime Minister. Finally, Ryerson University's name was changed to Toronto Metropolitan University.

DEATH OF THE INDIGENOUS WOMAN JOYCE ECHAQUAN – FRANCOIS LEGAULT DENIES SYSTEMIC RACISM IN QUEBEC

Systemic racism has a long history in the province of Quebec, but Premier of Quebec Francois Legault has continued to deny the presence of systemic racism in Quebec. He ran his 2018 campaign on controversial issues, including a ban on public servants wearing religious symbols such as the turban, kippa, cross, or headscarf. The legislation in Quebec, Bill 21, was widely criticized across Canada as discriminatory. Many other incidents, such as the attack on the Quebec Mosque in January 2017, killing six people, and the *death* of the Indigenous woman Joyce Echaquan in September 2020 in a Quebec hospital, are undeniable examples of systemic racism in Quebec.

A 37-year-old Indigenous lady, Joyce Echaquan, who was the mother of seven, died on September 28, 2020, in a Quebec hospital. The nurses were recorded screaming at her, "you're stupid as hell," only good at having sex, and "better off dead." The coroner said that racism and prejudice had played a role in her mistreatment and death, as the medical staff had erroneously attributed her symptoms to withdrawal from narcotics.

There were calls for the Quebec government to recognize "systemic racism" in the healthcare system and across the province. However, Quebec's premier, François Legault, refused to acknowledge the existence of systemic racism in Quebec. Mr. Legault openly said that there was no systemic racism in Quebec.

THE ILLEGAL CASINO SCANDAL

In October 2020, according to a police report, a mansion in the Greater Toronto Area was discovered to have a huge underground gambling den and supper club. When the police raided this place in July 2020, it was to be used as an illegal casino. The media reported that a Toronto real estate developer who owned this place met Justin Trudeau twice in 2016, along with the Chinese government-endorsed industry group. A member was also reported to have donated one million dollars to the Trudeau Foundation.

PAUL BUNNER, THE SPEECHWRITER FOR JASON KENNEY, CALLS RESIDENTIAL SCHOOLS A FAKE STORY

Paul Bunner, the speechwriter for Jason Kenney, the Premier of Alberta, had one of his articles from 2013 resurface, in which he called residential schools a fake genocide story. The article, "The Genocide That Failed," was published in 2013, in which Paul Bunner shares his views on residential schools and the intergenerational trauma of Indigenous communities. His article is filled with racist comments towards the Indigenous community. As his 2013 article was released, dozens of other articles he had written in the 1990s and 2000s resurfaced and were made public. These articles included his comments about women, minority groups, homeless populations, and Indigenous peoples. In 2000, Bunner wrote an article focusing on Canada's homeless community and how those individuals chose to live on the streets while the rest of Canada suffers due to their poor choices.

As these articles surfaced in 2020, Premier Kenney refused to fire Bunner as his speechwriter, despite Bunner's controversial comments. Although Kenney did not agree with him, he stood by Bunner's side, which raised questions about Kenney's position on racism. Indigenous leaders and other politicians called for his resignation, naming him unfit to participate in the government as he is discriminating against many minorities of the Canadian population. The Alberta Treaty Nation demanded his resignation as he had discriminated against all minority groups of Canada, including the victims of residential schools. After being under fire for months, Premier Jason Kenney's speechwriter, Paul Bunner, resigned from his position in September 2020.

JASON KENNEY ACCUSES THE SOUTH ASIAN COMMUNITY OF SPREADING COVID-19

In an interview with Calgary radio station Red 106.7FM in November 2020, Alberta Premier Jason Kenney delivered what he called a "wake-up call" to the community. He stated, "We see a very high level of spread of COVID-19 in the South Asian community. And I don't say that to blame or target anyone," Kenney said in the recorded interview with host Rishi Nagar.

These comments provoked frustration in Calgary's South Asian community, as these comments were perceived to be discriminatory. The South Asian community felt that Kenny was suggesting their large family gatherings were to blame for the rapid spread of the COVID-19 virus. Members of the community demanded an apology as Jason Kenney's statement narrated a demonstration of systemic racism. These minority communities have many immigrants who are doing jobs that cannot be performed from their homes, such as taxi drivers and janitors. Jason Kenney's comments targeted this community without understanding the factors driving the higher COVID-19 case numbers.

MP DEREK SLOAN REMOVED FROM THE CONSERVATIVE CAUCUS

Conservative MP Derek Sloan received nearly 15 percent of the votes on the first round of the Conservative Party of Canada's leadership race. He played a key role in the victory of Erin O'Toole. He was removed from the Conservative caucus in January 2021 because of receiving a donation from a white supremacist. Mr. Derek Sloan has raised questions about vaccinations. He ran as an independent candidate in the 2021 Alberta election and lost.

BLOC QUÉBÉCOIS LEADER BLANCHET'S COMMENTS ABOUT MINISTER OMAR ALGHABRA

In January 2021, Bloc Québécois Leader Yves-François Blanchet started raising suspicions about the Syrian Muslim identity of Canada's new transport minister, Omar Alghabra. Mr. Alghabra previously served as president of the Canadian Arab Federation (CAF) before being first elected to the House of Commons in 2006. Members of the Canadian Arab Federation (CAF) include Canadians of Arabic origin who are Muslim, Christian, or of any other faith. Blanchet criticized the legitimacy of Omar Alghabra and questioned Alghabra's connections to what Blanchet described as the "Political Islamic Movement." Prime Minister Trudeau called it playing dangerous games around intolerance and hate.

TORONTO MP EMPLOYING SISTER IN THE OFFICE

A Liberal MP, Yasmin Ratansi, from Toronto, had employed her sister in her constituency office using taxpayers' public funds, which is a violation of parliamentary rules. She admitted to a judgment error and had remedied the situation. In the spring of 2021, it was found that she violated the code of ethics by hiring her sister to work in her constituency office. She decided to sit as an Independent MP. Several former staffers disclosed that MP Ratansi had tried to cover up the violation by having her sister use a fake first name and not disclose the family connection. She did not run in the 2021 federal election.

BUDGET OF 2021

The 2021 federal budget placed significant focus on childcare support. As in Quebec, support for early childcare has long been sought in Canada. However, there were concerns about the program's delivery, particularly regarding negotiations with the provinces. Provinces may not be ready to participate in the federal government-designed program. Although support for early childcare was a good step, many Canadians wanted an approach that would allow parents to make their own childcare choices. Increasing the Canada Child Benefit would have given parents more flexibility, rather than investing in childcare.

There were new taxes on foreign-owned houses and vaping products. There were also concerns from the opposition about the sustainability of spending over time. There was no fiscal anchor in this budget, and taxes might be increased in the future. Due to significant overspending in the fiscal year 2020-2021, as planned by the liberal government, there may be economic overstimulation, inflation, a ballooning housing market, and rising interest rates, all of which may cause problems.

There was no clear path forward to address the challenges faced by people in Western Canada, particularly in Alberta. Alberta consistently had one of the highest unemployment rates, not only during the pandemic but also before it. This was seen as an election budget aimed at winning votes in Ontario, Quebec, and the rest of Eastern Canada, while Alberta workers in the energy, agriculture, and other sectors were left behind. This budget lacked the acknowledgement that the Alberta energy industry was part of any environmental plan. There was no support for training or retraining unemployed skilled workers affected by Alberta's energy sector crisis.

CANCELLATION OF THE KEYSTONE PIPELINE AND WESTERN ALIENATION

The news of the US President Joe Biden's 2021 cancellation of the Keystone pipeline was hailed by the Green Party and the NDP in Canada. A sentiment of Western Alienation increased with statements like "oil is dead" by some Canadian politicians. Calls to shut down the oil and gas industry only widened the divide between Eastern and Western Canada. Environmental groups have consistently opposed the oil and gas industry, creating additional barriers to Canada's ability to export its natural resources globally and to compete in international markets. These politicians and groups have been running a campaign that opposes the oil and gas industries and sidelines Canadian natural resources, which can jeopardize our economy by harming the oil and gas sector.

The National Energy Program (NEP) dismayed Albertans, who believed it gave the federal government special powers to intrude on provincial jurisdiction. The Albertans felt this way as the Canadian government was draining them of their natural wealth, and the eastern provinces were being subsidized at the expense of the western provinces. Many politicians have been demanding that the federal government not invest in Canada's oil and gas industry, claiming it is "dead." Youths have led demonstrations calling on the government to stop such investments.

ALLEGATIONS OF SEXUAL MISCONDUCT IN THE CANADIAN MILITARY

Many allegations of sexual misconduct against high-ranking military officers came to light in 2021. Canadians were asking for a full investigation of allegations of sexual misconduct. There were calls for the victims to deserve complete justice, while an announcement of another review of the military's culture would not bring much change.

Former Prime Minister Stephen Harper appointed General Vance in July 2015 when Erin O'Toole was

Minister of Veterans Affairs. At the time, General Vance was under active investigation by the Canadian Forces National Investigation Service. This raised several critical questions, such as what role did O'Toole and Harper play in the investigation of these allegations of sexual misconduct? When General Vance was appointed, why were the investigations suddenly dropped? Did the military police recommend ending the investigations immediately upon his appointment? Was the Commanding officer under pressure to end the probe? Who was putting pressure to end this probe?

Canadians were demanding a thorough investigation involving Erin O'Toole, Stephen Harper, Minister Sajjan, and the PMO of Prime Minister Justin Trudeau. Canadians wanted to know what role previous Conservative and current Liberal governments had played in investigating these serious allegations. After the 2021 Election, Defence Minister Sajjan was removed from his role.

DISCOVERY OF UNMARKED GRAVES OF INDIGENOUS CHILDREN IN KAMLOOPS, B.C

There was a discovery of unmarked graves of 215 children near the site of the former Kamloops residential school in May 2021. Leaders of the Tk'emlúps te Secwépemc Nation had requested Trudeau to visit the grieving community.

DISCOVERY OF UNMARKED GRAVES OF INDIGENOUS CHILDREN IN RESIDENTIAL SCHOOLS

The Cowessess First Nation announced a preliminary finding of 751 unmarked graves in June 2021, at a cemetery near the former Marieval Indian Residential School in Saskatchewan. This grim discovery added more to the intergenerational trauma and pain that are already being suffered by the First Nation communities.

The residential schools were a collective, calculated effort of churches and the government to eradicate Indigenous language and culture, which the Truth and Reconciliation Commission called a policy of cultural genocide. From 2008 to 2014, the Truth and Reconciliation Commission heard stories from thousands of residential school survivors. In June 2015, the commission released a report based on those hearings. From that came the 94 Calls to Action: individual instructions to guide governments, communities, and faith groups down the road to reconciliation.

$10 A DAY CHILDCARE PROGRAM

In April 2021, the Trudeau Liberal government announced to establish a Canada-wide childcare system. The Canadian parents will pay an average of $10 a day for childcare.

MURDER OF A MUSLIM FAMILY IN LONDON, ONTARIO

In June 2021, a Muslim family in London, Ontario, became the victims of a hate-motivated attack. In London, Ontario, Salman Afzaal, 46, his wife, who was 44, their 15-year-old daughter, and Salman Afzaal's 74-year-old mother were killed after a truck driver ran them over as they were taking an evening walk. The police reported that the driver of the truck planned the attack and targeted the family because of their Muslim faith. The youngest member of the family, a 9-year-old boy, survived but was seriously injured.

FEDERAL ELECTION 2021- THE MOST DIVISIVE CAMPAIGN

Although elections in Canada are supposed to be held every four years, Trudeau triggered an election, hoping the Liberals would win a majority government for their pandemic performance. The 2021 Canadian federal election was held on September 20, 2021, and Justin Trudeau won a third term as prime minister with the Liberal Party minority government. The results were mostly unchanged from the 2019 Election. The Liberals won 160 seats, short of the 170 seats needed for a majority government.

The campaign for this election created the most division in our society. People's Party leader Maxime Bernier was leading anti-lockdown marches in various cities. People were throwing stones at Justin Trudeau in various places, and he was unable to continue his campaign for several days.

2021 CABINET APPOINTMENTS

In these unprecedented times, as a nation, Canadians were not only dealing with the pandemic but were also facing an affordability and unity crisis. For a strong economic future, a strong government was needed, which was hard-working, committed, and honest. However, many ministers lacked a practical, rational approach to the problems. With inflation rising and the prices of daily necessities increasing, the government needed a responsible approach to fiscal management.

JUSTIN TRUDEAU WENT ON VACATION ON CANADA'S FIRST NATIONAL DAY FOR TRUTH AND RECONCILIATION

September 30th was the new federal holiday to honour the indigenous children who were forcefully admitted to the residential school system. On this first national day, Mr. Trudeau's daily schedule indicated that he would spend the day in private meetings in Ottawa; instead, he went on vacation with his family on the beach in Tofino, British Columbia. Many Indigenous leaders condemned his decision not to mark the day in person with the grieving families of the children who died in the residential schools and never came home. He was invited by Indigenous organizations, and he had turned down their invitation. Trudeau apologized for this later.

JUSTIN TRUDEAU CALLING ANTI-VAXXERS RACISTS, MISOGYNISTS

In an interview in September 2021, Mr. Trudeau called anti-vaxxers racists and misogynists. It was considered an attack on a subset of citizens and a blatant contempt, as Prime Minister Justin Trudeau showed in an angry tone during a French-language TV interview. He called these anti-vaxxers "often" being women-haters, racists, and science-deniers. This created backlash on social media.

CONSERVATIVES POSITION ON VACCINATION

Members of the Conservative caucus were divided on their approach to the mandated vaccinations. As of October 19th, 2021, a vaccine mandate was authorized, declaring that any individual entering the House of Commons should be fully vaccinated against the coronavirus. All individuals with access to the buildings were required to be fully vaccinated by November 22nd, 2021. Conservative Leader Erin O'Toole stated that the Conservative Party would "respect and abide" by the policy that was brought forward into the House of Commons. However, O'Toole further stated that the Conservative Party will be challenging the policy at the earliest opportunity available to them.

The objections to mandated vaccinations became evident within the Conservative caucus after MP Marilyn Gladu made remarks on the issue. On CTV's

Question Period, MP Gladu defended the unvaccinated community, arguing that individuals are being forced to disclose their vaccination status. This can lead to the enforcement of disclosure requirements for medical history, with no limitations on medical privacy. She also continued to compare COVID-19 to the Polio epidemic that spread in Canada in the first half of the 20th century. Some other members of the Conservative party shared their opinions regarding mandatory vaccinations, calling breach of privacy.

O'Toole acknowledged this division within the caucus, which only deepened public uncertainty. However, he disclosed that he would address this matter privately with his team.

ERIN O'TOOLE SUSPENDED BERT CHAN, THE NATIONAL COUNCIL MEMBER

In October 2021, the Conservative Party's national council member, Bert Chen, was also suspended after pushing the idea of early leadership review by starting an online petition.

ERIN O'TOOLE EXPELS THE SENATOR CALLING FOR LEADERSHIP REVIEW

A senator from Saskatchewan appointed by Stephen Harper suggested that conservatives should be able to vote within the next six months instead of 2023 to decide if O'Toole should remain the leader. In

November 2021, a day later, O'Toole removed Sen. Denise Batters from the conservative caucus. Conservative leader Erin O'Toole defended his decision to dismiss Senator Dennis Batters from the caucus, saying he will not tolerate an individual who discredits the efforts of the entire Conservative caucus, which is holding the corrupt and disastrous Trudeau government to account.

FIRING OF A TEACHER IN QUEBEC DUE TO BILL 21

Quebec Bill 21 was legislated in June 2019. As a result of this law, a teacher in Quebec was fired in December 2021 for wearing a headscarf, i.e., a hijab. Prime Minister Justin Trudeau was aware of this law and this incident. In fact, journalists questioned him several times if he would take any practical action against this discriminatory law. He has always given statements that did not reflect any real commitment on his part to end this law. During the English debate in the 2021 federal election, he was asked by the moderator about his opinion on Quebec's Bill 21. He remarked that the question was offensive to him and demanded an apology from the moderator for the question about this law.

As Prime Minister of Canada, it was his responsibility to defend the basic human rights of every Canadian citizen, not only on Canadian soil but also for Canadians abroad. Trudeau's statement that he did not want to interfere with this law was seen by many Canadians and minority communities as a failure of leadership and a lack of responsibility.

Trudeau has always attempted to present himself as a supporter of minorities, but racial minorities felt that he failed them on this issue. It became clear that his statements supporting racial minorities were just empty words, and his campaign of diversity and inclusion was nothing but fake. Trudeau has been fooling minorities with these false slogans. Racial minorities in Canada needed to reflect the betrayal and hypocrisy of Trudeau.

The statements of backbencher MPs from Ontario who had a significant number of constituents from racial communities were meaningless. These statements were nothing more than an attempt to pacify their voters. These MPs should have questioned the Prime Minister in the House of Commons as to why he did not challenge this law in the Supreme Court of Canada. Since these MPs were part of the Liberal Party, it was their duty to raise this issue with the Liberal Government, as racial minorities have always supported the Liberal Party.

Many Human Rights Associations condemned the utter lack of concern, inaction, irresponsible behaviour, and indifference that Mr. Trudeau had displayed regarding Quebec Bill 21. He failed to protect the basic human rights of Canadians as set out in the Canadian Charter of Rights and Freedoms.

TRUCKERS CONVEY IN OTTAWA

Justin Trudeau's government faced the challenge of COVID-19. Although Canada managed it better than its southern neighbour, there were thousands of deaths, especially among long-term care home residents who were affected. The government had to follow the public health department's advice to impose restrictions on physical distancing, lockdowns, facial masks, and mandatory vaccinations. These measures were perceived both ways. Some Canadians thought that border controls, lockdowns, and other restrictions should have been stricter, whereas others opposed them. Canada had a generally unified approach to the pandemic, and almost 85 percent of the population was vaccinated. Overall, Canadians were far more united in their response to COVID-19 than Americans.

In 2021, many right-wing conservative politicians started campaigning against these measures. This led to the rise of public sentiment against these restrictions, especially at the beginning of 2022. The trucker vaccination mandate was the tipping point that sparked protests by a small but vocal minority. There was a Truckers Convoy that protested in Ottawa and in many other cities across the country in January 2022. This convoy of Truckers was from across Canada. They proclaimed to be "The Freedom Convoy" and came to Ottawa on January 28, 2022, to protest the federal vaccine mandate for truckers, which required Canadian truck drivers crossing the US border to be fully vaccinated. Soon, this evolved into a protest against all public health measures related to the COVID-19 pandemic. Some media reports indicated that convoy members had believed in the misinformation and fake controversies. There were media reports that Fox News had been fanning the same flames about this conspiracy as on January 6th, 2021, the Capitol Hill attack.

Although this protest started peacefully to express opinion against vaccine mandates for truckers, many undesirable acts were reported by the protestors, including harassing healthcare workers, honking, waving confederate flags and swastikas, taking food from homeless people and food banks, and interfering with local businesses. The healthcare workers were advised not to wear their scrubs or display any work-related identity to avoid harassment on their way to hospitals or other healthcare institutions. The convoy not only blocked many streets in downtown Ottawa but also the Ambassador Bridge in Windsor, affecting hundreds of millions of dollars in trade with the USA every single day.

Many Conservative politicians, including MPs and the leader of the opposition, supported the trucking convoy and met the protesters in person. Some key organizers of the Truckers Convoy were attempting to overthrow Trudeau's government and asking for the resignation of the Prime Minister and nominate a citizens' government. Conservative Party leadership candidate and MP Pierre Poilievre said he was proud of them. The leader of the opposition and interim leader of the Conservative Party, Candice Bergen, was calling protesters "passionate, patriotic & peaceful." Former Conservative Party leader Andrew Scheer took pictures with convoy members, and Alberta MP Michael Cooper also met the convoy and endorsed their protest. Prime Minister Justin Trudeau said that Conservatives have been endorsing and enabling these blockades across the country.

The protesters were flooding Ottawa's 9-1-1 emergency system with crank calls. This caused public distress. Many Canadians felt that the Conservative leadership was igniting the protest. Conservative leader Candice Bergen and MPs were calling on the government to drop all vaccine mandates, despite public health professionals' advice to the contrary. Many people felt that Conservatives should stand with the government, not with protesters, because it would set a precedent that any group could block our supply chain illegally and change policies. This would only hurt our democratic traditions and institutions.

Conservative politicians supported the protesters from the back door to paralyze the government so that the government would have no options but to use force, which could lead to casualties. This was considered an example of hyper-partisanship. In this time of crisis, the opposition and the government should have worked together as one team to save our democracy and send a strong message that both are on the same page. Alberta and Saskatchewan Premiers Jason Kenney and Scot Moe suddenly announced to lift restrictions on vaccine mandates, which made the federal government look authoritarian.

This protest caused a great division in Canadian society. Many people on social media were calling the protestors terrorists, racists, and white supremacists, whereas the interim leader of the Conservative Party and leader of the opposition, Candice Bergen, said about protesters, "there are good people on both sides." Courts issued injunctions to remove the protest, a heavy police presence was deployed, and RCPM were sent to the protest sites to clear the Ambassador Bridge. The opposition blamed Justin Trudeau for dividing the public due to these restrictions.

JUSTIN TRUDEAU INVOKED THE FEDERAL WAR MEASURES ACT FIRST TIME CANADIAN HISTORY.

The government did not engage in any dialogue with the protestors, and on February 14th, 2022, Justin Trudeau invoked the Emergency Measures Act in Canada. This created a lot of controversy in public.

ERIN O'TOOLE REMOVED FROM LEADERSHIP OF THE CONSERVATIVE PARTY

In January 2022, Mr. Erin O'Toole was removed from leadership of the Conservative Party by the Conservative caucus, and Candice Bergen became

Leader of the Opposition and the interim leader of the Conservative Party. Her pictures wearing a baseball cap with the inscription "Make America Great Again " over a camouflage background were circulating on social media. She and many other conservative politicians have supported the Truckers Freedom Convoy.

QUEBEC IMPOSING TAX ON UNVACCINATED

Francois Legault announced in January 2022 that he would impose a tax on unvaccinated Quebecers. Although this is against Canada's public health policies, the federal government has not taken a clear position on it. This was opposed by many politicians across the country. This decision was later cancelled.

QUEBEC BILL 96 BECAME LAW

Quebec Bill 96 was passed by the Quebec Assembly in June 2022. Its aim was to establish French as the official and common language of Quebec. The Quebec government proposed an overhaul of its French-language charter with Bill 96, described as an update to Bill 101, the province's French-language charter first adopted in 1977. Many concerns were raised about its impact on English-speaking communities and on the independence of the judiciary. During the English-language debate in the 2021 federal election campaign, Bill 96 and Bill 21 in Quebec were described as discriminatory legislation.

Bill 96 indicated a unilateral change to the Canadian Constitution, affirming Quebec as a separate nation and French as its only official language. In addition, many other amendments to this law aimed at strengthening the status of French, including tougher sign laws, more language requirements for businesses, and less access to English in junior colleges. The Quebec government invoked the notwithstanding clause to avoid any charter challenges. Quebec Community Groups called for the withdrawal of the bill. This Bill could prompt other provinces to follow suit by unilaterally changing the Canadian Constitution, further dividing the country.

FIGHT ON HYBRID PARLIAMENT SESSIONS

Conservative MPs opposed the hybrid format of meetings in the House of Commons during the pandemic, whereas Liberal and NDP MPs supported hybrid parliamentary sessions. This had allowed MPs to participate virtually in the House of Commons' sessions during the pandemic. The Conservatives and the Bloc Québécois argued against the hybrid sessions in October 2022. The Conservatives stated that hybrid sessions will allow the government to be "off the hook" and to avoid answering questions in parliament. Conservative deputy leader Candice Bergen maintained that the government is protected from "scrutiny and accountability" by hybrid sessions. The leader of the House of Commons explained that a hybrid format within the House will provide flexibility for MPs amid the difficult circumstances of the pandemic.

PIERRE POILIEVRE ELECTED LEADER OF THE CONSERVATIVE PARTY

In January 2022, Mr. Erin O'Toole was removed from leadership of the Conservative Party by the vote of the Conservative caucus. In a leadership contest, Ontario MP and former Cabinet minister in Harper's Conservative government, Pierre Poilievre, was elected with 68 percent of the available points on the first ballot. Jean Charest, former Quebec Premier, was second. Other candidates were MP Leslyn Lewis, MP Scott Aitchison, and Ontario MPP Roman Baber. Former leader of the Progressive Conservative Party of Ontario and Brampton Mayor Patrick Brown was disqualified in early July due to alleged campaign violations.

TRUDEAU'S BOHEMIAN RHAPSODY SINGING BEFORE QUEEN'S FUNERAL

In 2022, Justin Trudeau was criticized for singing "Bohemian Rhapsody" in a hotel lobby in London, United Kingdom, a couple of days before Queen Elizabeth II's funeral. He was dressed in a maroon t-shirt and dark jeans, and other members of the Canadian delegation to the funeral were also present. This video became viral immediately.

NPD AND LIBERAL CONFIDENCE-AND-SUPPLY AGREEMENT

On March 22, 2022, the New Democratic Party entered into a confidence-and-supply agreement with the Liberal minority government. This agreement was intended to keep the minority Liberal government in power until 2025, with the NDP agreeing to support the government on confidence motions and budget votes. In exchange, the Liberal government pledged to advance work on key New Democratic Party policy priorities, including dental care, pharmacare, and affordable childcare. The Liberal-NDP government introduced national pharmacare and dental care programs. New Democratic Party leader Jagmeet Singh announced the early termination of the agreement on September 4th, 2024.

LIBERAL MP ATTENDING PARLIAMENT SESSION WITH HIS PANTS DOWN IN THE WASHROOM

In May 2022, an Ontario Liberal MP, Shafqat Ali, was allegedly caught sitting in the bathroom while attending a virtual session of the House of Commons. Conservative MP Laila Goodridge raised a point of order and said that the Liberal MP for Brampton Centre "might be participating in a washroom."

Assistant Deputy Speaker Alexandra Mendès confirmed that the Liberal MP "appeared to be in the washroom" with his pants down while participating in a debate on Bill C-252.

LIBERALS ANNOUNCED STRENGTHENING GUN CONTROL

In May 2022, Justin Trudeau announced new legislation to improve gun control. The aim of Bill C-21 was to keep Canadians safe from gun violence. Some of the measures include implementing a national freeze on buying, selling, and transferring handguns, taking away the firearms licenses of those involved in domestic violence, stopping gun smuggling and trafficking by increasing criminal penalties, and creating a new "red flag" law that would enable courts to require those people considered a danger to self or others to surrender their firearms. The police chiefs, families of survivors, physicians, and trauma surgeons were asking for these concrete actions. This created concerns among legal gun owners, and conservative politicians were in strong opposition of these measures.

TRUDEAU STICKS OUT HIS TONGUE IN THE PARLIAMENT

In 2023, Justin Trudeau was criticized for sticking out his tongue and winking at newly elected Speaker Greg Fergus. This video became viral immediately. Speaker Fergus introduced Trudeau as the "honourable Prime Minister" before his address, and Justin Trudeau made a light-hearted comment, calling himself "very honourable".

LIBERAL MP MARY NG SCANDAL.

In February 2023, International Trade and Small Business Minister Mary Ng was found to award contracts for media training and public relations work to Amanda Alvaro, a communications professional and Power & Politics panellist. This was found to constitute a breach of federal conflict-of-interest laws. Mary Ng was reprimanded by the ethics commissioner for failing to recuse herself from the contracting process.

ARRIVECAN APP SCANDAL

The ArriveCAN app was developed in April 2020 as a COVID-19 screening tool, and travellers entering Canada were required to upload their contact, travel, and quarantine information. It was mandatory for all travellers entering Canada from November 2020 until October 1st, 2022. It was initially estimated to cost $80,000. There was much controversy over how much this app cost, and some reports suggested the federal government might have spent approximately $ 54 million on it, with more than 20 subcontractors. The federal government refused to submit contracting documents due to concerns of confidentiality. In October 2022, two IT companies claimed they could develop a similar app for approximately $250,000. On November 2nd, 2022, a motion was passed calling on the

Auditor General of Canada to conduct a performance audit for all aspects of the ArriveCAN app.

CHINESE GOVERNMENT INTERFERENCE

In February 2023, CSIS reported that the Chinese government interfered in the 2019 and 2021 elections. Opposition political parties demanded a public inquiry.

In May 2023, Canada expelled Chinese diplomat Zhao Wei, accusing him of intimidating a Canadian politician. Justin Trudeau nominated former Governor General of Canada David Johnston to investigate these allegations. Johnston filed an interim report, describing China's interference as a threat to our democracy, and recommended several measures to counter it. The opposition called for a full judicial inquiry, but Johnston recommended against it. He was supposed to continue his inquiry with public hearings, with a conclusion in October 2023, but instead resigned as the special rapporteur in June 2023.

In September 2023, Justin Trudeau asked Québec Justice Marie-Josée Hogue to preside over the public inquiry into Foreign Interference in Federal Electoral Processes and Democratic Institutions. In May 2024, preliminary findings were reported that China engaged in foreign interference in both elections, but it did not affect the result of either election.

MURDER OF A CANADIAN CITIZEN IN B.C

The prime minister's national security advisor warned that India was involved in foreign interference in Canada. It was revealed in Parliament by Prime Minister Justin Trudeau that India was involved in the killing of a Canadian citizen, Hardeep Singh Nijjar, in B.C in June 2023. Conservative MPs, including Pierre Poilievre and Andrew Scheer, reacted very strongly in support of the Indian government and raised doubts about these allegations.

MILLION MARCH ACROSS CANADA AGAINST INDOCTRINATION AND GENDER IDEOLOGY

On September 20th, 2023, Canadian parents and concerned citizens held a 1 Million March from coast to coast. People of different religions, ethnicities, atheists, and those with various political ideologies marched against the radical gender ideology and the sexualization of Canadian children. Protests were held peacefully in St. John's, Charlottetown, Halifax, Fredericton, Montreal, Ottawa, Toronto, London, Ontario, Edmonton, Calgary, Vancouver, and many other cities, with one message: "Leave our kids alone!" NDP leader Jagmeet Singh led a counter-protest against this parental march. Prime Minister Justin Trudeau also issued harsh statements against the protests.

YAROSLAV HUNKA SANDAL - SPEAKER RESIGNS

On September 22nd, 2023, during Ukrainian President Volodymyr Zelenskyy's visit to Canada, Ukrainian-Canadian veteran Yaroslav Hunka was honoured with a standing ovation by Speaker Anthony Rota. He was praised as a hero of Canada and Ukraine. Later, it was revealed that Hunka had been a member of the Waffen-SS Galicia Division, which was under the command of the Nazis. Both opposition and Liberal MPs condemned this as irresponsible and unacceptable, leading to Speaker Anthony Rota's resignation.

MPP SARA JAMA REMOVED FROM ONTARIO NDP CAUCUS

Although NDP Leader Marit Stiles said in a statement that the caucus allows different viewpoints, in October 2023, an Ontario MPP from Hamilton Centre was kicked out of the NDP caucus for a social media post in support of Palestinians. Jama, 29-year-old disability and housing advocate, won her seat in a byelection.

CONSERVATIVES OBJECT TO ALLEGATIONS OF INDIAN INVOLVEMENT IN THE KILLING OF A CANADIAN CITIZEN

Conservative MPs, including Andrew Scheer, objected to the allegation that Indian officials were involved in the killing of Hardeep Nijjar. They claimed that this allegation would only worsen the relationship with India. They also said that the relations between India and Canada had been strained since Justin Trudeau alleged India's involvement in the killing of Hardeep Singh Nijjar. India refuted these claims.

INDIAN INTERFERENCE IN THE CONSERVATIVE PARTY LEADERSHIP RACE

Agents of the Indian government were reported to have interfered in the Conservative Party's leadership race in 2022. They purchased memberships for one candidate and opposed the other. They appeared to be funding a number of politicians at all levels of government, as reported by CSIS. These allegations came from an October 2022 CSIS Intelligence Assessment, which included election interference by China and India. Several media reports claimed that a Conservative MP, Arpan Khanna, might be under investigation by CSIS for potentially receiving support from the government of India in a nomination race. He was also Poilievre's Ontario co-chair during this leadership race. There were some media reports that India interfered to support Pierre Poilievre in the 2022 Conservative leadership contest.

PHARMACARE BY THE LIBERAL GOVERNMENT

In February 2024, the federal Liberal government and the NDP reached an agreement on pharmacare as part of their confidence-and-supply agreement. Medications for Diabetes and contraceptives were included in this package.

NATIONAL SCHOOL FOOD PROGRAM

In April 2024, the Liberal government announced a National School Food Program. Prime Minister Justin Trudeau announced in the 2024 budget that the government would provide meals to more children in schools to help them access healthy food and improve their health, learning, and education.

DENTAL CARE PROGRAM

In May 2024, the Liberal government launched a dental care program to provide oral health insurance to those with a household income of less than $90,000. This was designed for people who were not covered through private insurance. This was also part of the agreement between the NDP and Liberal government. The estimated cost of this program was about $13 billion over five years. Seniors aged 87, adults receiving disability benefits, and children under 18 are eligible, and about 9 million people without dental coverage are expected to benefit from this program.

LIBERALS LOST THEIR LONGTIME SEAT IN TORONTO

In June 2024, Liberals lost one of the safest seats in a byelection in Toronto. Trudeau remained adamant that he would stay in office amid fresh questions about his future.

LIBERALS LOST THEIR LONGTIME SEAT IN THE BY-ELECTION IN MONTREAL

In September 2024, the Bloc Québécois won a by-election in the LaSalle-Émard-Verdun riding in Montreal, a longtime Liberal seat.

NDP WITHDRAWS ITS SUPPORT FROM LIBERAL GOVERNMENT

In September 2024, the New Democratic Party, which had been propping up the Liberal minority government, decided to withdraw its support. The Trudeau Liberals had only one choice of getting support of the Bloc Québécois.

PIERRE POILIEVRE REFUSES SECURITY CLEARANCE

In October 2024, during testimony before the inquiry, Justin Trudeau said he had seen the names of Conservative politicians engaged in foreign interference. He further stated that he advised CSIS to pass that information to Mr. Poilievre, but CSIS was unable to do so without Poilievre first obtaining security clearance. Trudeau said the leader of the opposition's decision not to obtain the necessary clearance to obtain those names and to protect the integrity of his party did not make sense. Trudeau also said he was aware that members of other parties, including his own, were vulnerable to foreign interference. However, the leader of the opposition, Pierre Poilievre, refused to obtain the security clearance.

Justin Trudeau spoke regarding Pierre Poilievre's response to foreign interference: "It is so egregious to me that the leader of the official opposition, who is certainly trying very hard to become prime minister, is choosing to play partisan games with foreign interference." Trudeau said Pierre Poilievre should receive a security clearance so he can receive a briefing on top-secret and classified information regarding his party and some of its members. Poilievre said that Trudeau was lying and called on him to release the names of politicians allegedly involved.

LIBERAL MINISTER MARY NG IS SUPPORTED BY THE CHINESE GOVERNMENT

In October of 2024, CSIS investigations identified that Mary Ng was one of eleven Toronto-area candidates clandestinely supported by the Chinese government.

TRUMP PLEDGED 25% TARIFFS ON IMPORTS FROM CANADA

In November 2024, US President-elect Donald Trump said that, upon taking office in January 2025, he would impose a 25% tariff on all products imported into the United States from Canada and Mexico.

TRUMP WANTS TO MAKE CANADA A US STATE

President-elect Donald Trump, in his multiple statements, said he would like to make Canada a state of the USA. He referred to Justin Trudeau as Governor Trudeau. He also said he will use economic force to overtake Canada. This was condemned by all major political leaders of Canada.

QUEBEC PREMIER ANNOUNCES BAN ON PRAYING

In December 2024, Quebec Premier François Legault said he would ban public prayer and would use the notwithstanding clause if necessary. He was giving an overview of the past year in Quebec City and said he has instructed his team to investigate ways to implement the ban on praying. He also commented about some teachers communicating among themselves and with students in Arabic. He said he has seen teachers implementing Islamist religious concepts in schools.

LIBERALS LOST ANOTHER BY-ELECTION IN BC

Liberals lost another seat in a byelection in B.C on December 16th, 2024, in the riding of Cloverdale-Langley. Conservatives won this seat on the same day that Justin Trudeau was facing calls to resign after Finance Minister Chrystia Freeland's resignation. Tamara Jansen was an MP from 2019 to 2021. This was the third seat the Liberals lost in a 2024 byelection.

TRUDEAU'S FINANCE MINISTER RESIGNS

On December 16th, 2024, Justin Trudeau's Deputy Prime Minister and Finance Minister, Chrystia Freeland, announced her resignation from cabinet on the day she was supposed to deliver a fall economic statement. Chrystia Freeland was one of Trudeau's most trusted ministers, but she said she and Trudeau have been at odds over government spending and how to handle possible US tariffs.

TRUDEAU'S MPS WANT HIM TO STEP DOWN

On December 17th, 2024, several Liberal MPs reportedly said that Justin Trudeau cannot continue as party leader following Chrystia Freeland's public resignation from cabinet. Trudeau told these MPs at a caucus meeting that he had heard their concerns and would take time to reflect on his future.

NDP ANNOUNCE TO FILE A NON-CONFIDENCE MOTION

On December 20th, 2024, NDP leader Jagmeet Singh announced that he would file a motion of no-confidence once the House of Commons returns after the winter break in January 2025. Mr. Yves-François Blanchet, leader of the Bloc Québécois, also announced his support for the non-confidence motion against Justin Trudeau.

TRUDEAU ANNOUNCED HIS RESIGNATION

On January 5th, 2025, Justin Trudeau announced that he would step down as leader of the Liberal Party. He prorogued the Parliament until March 24th, 2025. The new leader of the Liberal Party and prime minister will lead the party in the next federal election.

PROROGATION OF PARLIAMENT WAS CHALLENGED IN THE FEDERAL COURT

In January 2025, the prorogation of Parliament was challenged in the Federal Court, citing a reference on the prorogation of Parliament by Prime Minister Boris Johnson of the United Kingdom, which was overturned by the United Kingdom Court.

THE LIBERAL PARTY STARTED THE PROCESS OF ELECTING A NEW LEADER

The Liberal Party has started the process of electing a new leader who will be the next prime minister and lead the Liberal Party into the next elections. Mark Carney and Chrystia Freeland were strong candidates for this leadership role.

ALBERTA PREMIER DANIELLE SMITH MEETS TRUMP

In January 2025, Alberta Premier Danielle Smith met Trump in Florida. Premier Smith said that she had friendly and constructive conversations with Trump. She said she emphasized the U.S.-Canadian energy relationship and how American jobs are supported by energy exports from Alberta. Smith also announced that she would attend Trump's inauguration in Washington on January 20, whereas other Premiers handled the issue very differently. Ontario Premier Ford spoke forcefully against the tariffs and Trump's threat to make Canada the 51st state.

TRUMP POSTPONED TARIFFS ON CANADA UNTIL FEBRUARY 1ST, 2025

Trump did not announce 25% Tariffs on Canadian imports to the US on the day of taking office, postponing it until February 1st, 2025.

ONTARIO PREMIER FORD THREATENED TO CUT OFF ELECTRICITY TO THE US

In March 2025, Ontario Premier Doug Ford threatened to cut off electricity export to Michigan, New York, and Minnesota. This was in response to tariffs imposed by Trump. Ford said almost 1.5 million people in the US border states depend upon the Ontario power supply. This could affect manufacturing in the US, and Ford encouraged Quebec, Manitoba, and British Columbia to take the same steps. Ford also indicated that Ontario should stop exporting nickel, which could affect uranium supply in the US.

MARK CARNEY BECOMES LEADER OF THE LIBERAL PARTY AND PRIME MINISTER OF CANADA

On March 9th, 2025, Mark Carney, a former central banker, won the race to become the leader of the Liberal Party to replace Justin Trudeau. He took 86% of the votes on the first ballot to beat former Finance Minister Chrystia Freeland. He was sworn in at Rideau Hall in Ottawa on March 14th as the 24th Prime Minister of Canada.

MARK CARNEY CANCELLED CONSUMER CARBON TAX

After being sworn in, Prime Minister Mark Carney signed a prime ministerial directive to remove the carbon tax effective April 1st. He said, "This will make a difference to hard-pressed Canadians, but it is part of a much bigger set of measures that this government is taking to ensure that we fight against climate change, that our companies are competitive, and the country moves forward." He also said that the carbon tax had become a divisive issue.

TRUMP IMPOSED 25% TARIFFS ON CANADA

Trump imposed 25 percent tariffs on March 4th on imports from Canada, but he limited the levy to 10 percent on Canadian energy. Canadian Prime Minister Justin Trudeau announced tariffs on more than USD 100 billion in American goods.

Trump granted a one-month pause on his new tariffs on goods from Mexico and Canada for US automakers after speaking with the automakers' leaders.

TRUMP CONTINUES HIS "51ST. STATE" REMARKS

Trump continues to say Canada should become the 51st state of the US. This causes more division in Canada. Trump supporters in Canada continue to support him, but the majority of Canadians feel very annoyed.

LIBERALS CATCH UP TO CONSERVATIVES IN PUBLIC OPINION POLLS.

After Mark Carney became the Prime Minister, the Liberal Party began to rise in the polls. Carney began to move the Liberal Party closer to the political center. Because of his extensive experience as an economist, many Canadians felt he was better suited to address Canada's economic situation.

FEDERAL ELECTION, 2025

The 2025 Canadian federal election was held on April 28th, 2025. The main issues of the election campaign included the cost of living, housing, crime, US tariffs on Canadian exports, and threats of Donald Trump's annexation of Canada.

The Liberal Party won a fourth term, with a minority government. The Conservative Party improved upon its seat count from 2021, whereas the NDP won only seven seats and lost official party status for the first time since 1993. Jagmeet Singh, leader of the NDP, lost his own seat as well.

CONSERVATIVE LEADER PIERRE POILIEVRE LOSES HIS OWN SEAT

Conservative Leader Pierre Poilievre lost his long-held seat in the Ottawa area to a Liberal candidate.

PIERRE POILIEVRE RUNS FROM ALBERTA AND RETURNS TO THE HOUSE OF COMMONS.

A Conservative MP decided to resign so that Pierre Poilievre could run from Alberta. This was a very secure Conservative riding, and Pierre Poilievre won without any difficulty, becoming MP.

CONSERVATIVE PARTY GOES DOWN IN POLLS

However, despite winning this seat, Pierre Poilievre and the Conservative Party continued to fall in the polls. Several factors might have played a role, including negativity seen in his discussion in the House of Commons, his rhetoric of Canada being broken, a weak response to Trump's threats, a lack of condemnation of genocide in Gaza in the Middle East conflict, endorsing wars, and the very high profile of Mark Carney in the field of economics.

TRUMP CALLED CARNEY THE PRESIDENT OF CANADA.

In October 2025, Trump referred to Carney as the "president" of Canada at the "Summit for Peace," an international meeting to support a permanent ceasefire in Gaza. Trump said it was "so great" to have Canada on board. Trump said that Canada's "president" had called him, knowing "the importance" of the project.

Carney joked with Trump, saying he had "upgraded" him to president. Trump smiled and said, "At least I didn't say, governor."

CONSERVATIVE MPS FLOOR CROSSING

Reports of disagreements among various conservative MPs with their leadership began surfacing in the media as Pierre Poilievre continued to decline in the polls. An MP from Nova Scotia crossed the floor from Conservative to Liberal. This was followed by Michael Ma, MP for Markham, Ontario, who crossed the floor from the Conservative Party to the Liberal Party.

ANDREW SCHEER "BARGED" INTO OFFICE, MP CROSSING THE FLOOR

Andrew Scheer "barged" into the office of MP D'Entremont and started yelling at him about "how much of a snake" he was, shortly before MP D'Entremont crossed the floor to join the Liberal Party. Chris D'Entremont, the Nova Scotia MP, stated that after rumours of his crossing the floor surfaced, Andrew Scheer and another Conservative MP entered his office, pushed the door open, almost knocking over his assistant, and started yelling at him. He also described the atmosphere in the Conservative Party as a "frat house."

LIBERALS CLOSER TO MAJORITY

MP Michael Ma crossed the floor from the Conservative Party to join the Liberal Party, stating that he made the decision because it's "time for unity and decisive action rather than division." Floor crossing by MP D'Entremont and MP Ma brought the Liberal government closer to a majority.

CARNEY LIBERALS PASSED THE NOVEMBER 2025 BUDGET

Mark Carney's minority government budget passed a third and crucial confidence vote. MPs voted to approve the Liberal government's budget, and the budget motion passed 170 to 168. Two NDP MPs and two Conservative MPs abstained from voting. Green Party leader May also voted in support of the budget. Failure to pass the budget could trigger the election. Many media reports suggested that Conservatives also wanted the budget to pass, since Andrew Scheer and another MP joined late, after making sure the budget would pass, they might have abstained. Canadians at large and most political parties were not ready for another election.

CARNEY VISITS EUROPE, THE UAE AND OTHER COUNTRIES TO DEVELOP TRADE RELATIONS

Amid US tariffs and a trade war, Mark Carney continued exploring new trade partners. Carney's government wants to increase non-US exports and attract new investments in Canada. As part of this plan, Mark Carney visited the United Arab Emirates (UAE), where he developed new trade relationships by securing agreements to attract foreign investment. The two countries signed the new Canada-UAE Foreign Investment Promotion and Protection Agreement (FIPA) to foster a long-term partnership between Canadian and UAE industries. They are also negotiating toward a Comprehensive Economic Partnership Agreement (CEPA) to cut tariffs, eliminate red tape, and expand market access for Canadian exporters of goods and services.

ALBERTA SEPARATION PETITION GETS APPROVAL

A petition aiming for a referendum on Alberta's separation from Canada met the requirements under the Citizen Initiative Act. This petition asks, "Do you agree that the province of Alberta should cease to be a part of Canada to become an independent state?" The proponent must submit all petition signature sheets to Elections Alberta on or before May 2nd, 2026, and

Elections Alberta will verify the petition within 21 days of submission.

TRUMP ATTACKS VENEZUELA, KIDNAPPING ITS PRESIDENT AND HIS WIFE

On January 3rd, 2026, the United States launched a military strike on Venezuela and kidnapped Venezuelan President Nicolás Maduro and his wife, Cilia Flores. The US armed forces began the attack around 2 a.m. local time by bombing across northern Venezuela and attacking Maduro's compound in Caracas. President Maduro and his wife were transported to New York prison to face US federal criminal charges. Trump announced that the US will run Venezuela. The US government announced that Maduro was indicted on several charges related to narcoterrorism. Maduro pleaded not guilty to the charges in a Manhattan federal court on January 5th, 2026. During this attack, 75 Venezuelan security officers were reported to be killed. The United Nations (UN) said the raid violated international law, the UN Charter, and Venezuela's sovereignty.

PIERRE POILIEVRE CONGRATULATES TRUMP ON VENEZUELA ATTACK

Conservative Party leader Pierre Poilievre congratulated Trump on the attack on Venezuela and the kidnapping of its president, Maduro, and his wife. Many international law experts and journalists saw this as an endorsement of dismantling the very international order that keeps small countries and the world safe. Trump's motivation is not the liberation of the people of Venezuela but its oil. Trump has already said that American firms will revitalize Venezuela's 300 billion barrels of oil reserves. This attack set a precedent for "might is right," and the superpower can unilaterally invade a sovereign nation, declaring the end of international order. Many perceived Poilievre's congratulations as eroding Canada's moral standing to condemn Russia's invasion of Ukraine. Poilievre's position on this issue showed Canadians which side of the rules-based order he truly stands on. Poilievre's statements marked a departure from the traditional approach of past Canadian leaders, who have always remained committed to multilateral institutions that protect middle powers.

CARNEY APPLAUDED THE KIDNAPPING OF THE PRESIDENT OF VENEZUELA

Carney asked all parties to respect international law while applauding the illegal kidnapping and removal of a head of state of a sovereign nation by a foreign country. Caney cited the deaths of civilians and the authoritative policies of Mudaro. Careny's response to Trump's attack on Venezuela was criticized by many legal experts. Many senior practitioners of International Law said that if international law isn't applied to everyone, then it doesn't exist, and if there are exemptions to the rule of law, then there is no rule of law. Carney's reluctance to condemn Trump's attack on Venezuela sparked criticism from those who believe in international law. Careny was seen to endorse the idea that might makes right.

TRUMP'S ATTACK ON VENEZUELA AND CANADIANS

Canadians at large and specifically legal experts condemned the kidnapping of the President of Venezuela and his wife to face a trial in New York. Such actions are a clear violation of international law. Many Canadians were discussing how they would feel if the Prime Minister of Canada were kidnapped one night from his residence in Ottawa. Many Canadians were thinking that Canada could be subject to Trump's aggression at any time since he has been claiming to annex Canada as the 51st. state since he got elected. People criticized the Conservative Party leader's statement congratulating Trump on this action. Even those who liked Trump when he was running for a second term did not like his attack on Venezuela.

ALBERTA SEPARATISTS MEET THE TRUMP ADMINISTRATION

The Alberta separation movement is gaining momentum. Some media outlets reported that Jeff Rath, who is involved with the Alberta Prosperity Project, which supports Alberta's separation, and other members of the group, met with U.S. State Department officials in Washington in January to gauge the U.S. administration's response to an independent Alberta. The idea of a new pipeline from Alberta to the U.S. was also shared with U.S. officials. Many Canadians who oppose separation consider it foreign interference by the US. They think the Trump administration is interested in taking over Alberta only because of its rich resources, including oil and natural gas. Many fear that if separatists lose in the referendum, they will claim rigging, and the US administration will get involved to help separatists against the Canadian government, using the context of injustice.

US TREASURY SECRETARY SCOTT BESSENT ON THE ALBERTA SEPARATIST MOVEMENT

US Treasury Secretary Scott Bessent commented on the Alberta separatist movement by saying the western Canadian province is a "natural partner for the US". He said,

"Alberta has a wealth of natural resources, but they won't let them build a pipeline to the Pacific," During an interview in the US, he said, "I think we should let them come down into the US, and Alberta is a natural partner for the US. They have great resources. The Albertans are very independent people." He further said there is a "rumour that they may have a referendum on whether they want to stay in Canada or not". While a group in Alberta is collecting signatures for a referendum campaign, this was considered foreign interference in Canada.

TRUMP THREATENS TO TAKE OVER GREENLAND

Trump has repeatedly said that the US wants to annex Greenland with the option of military action despite the opposition from Greenlandic lawmakers. Trump has said that if the US does not take over, Russia or China will take over Greenland, and he does not want to allow Russia or China as a neighbour. He has said he would like to make a deal in an easy way, but if it is not possible, he will do it the hard way. Greenland is part of Denmark, with its own elected government and control over its internal affairs and natural resources, but Denmark still handles finance, defence, and foreign policy.

Since 2009, Greenland has also had the right to secede if its population votes for independence. Denmark has repeatedly said that Greenland is not for sale. Almost 85 percent of Greenland's population opposes joining the US. The US attack to annex Greenland would be a direct violation of the NATO treaty, and Denmark has said any such attack would end the military alliance. Trump says he needs Greenland from a national security perspective. There is a US military base in the northwestern corner of Greenland. Trump says Greenland is covered with Russian and Chinese ships all over the place; however, there is no evidence of their ships anywhere near Greenland. Greenland is also rich in minerals and rare earth metals, and it may have large oil and gas reserves.

CANADA CONTINUES TO GIVE AID TO UKRAINE

Canada announces $2 billion more in military aid to Ukraine for 2026–27. Since February 2022, Canada has committed more than $25 billion CAD in aid to Ukraine, including economic, military, and humanitarian support. Public opinion has been divided over such massive aid to Ukraine, as Canadians face affordability issues, housing shortages, and healthcare crises.

EUROPE AND CANADA STAND WITH DENMARK AGAINST THE US

Many European leaders, including Prime Minister Mark Carney, warned the US against annexing Greenland. Carney said, "Our full partnership and obligations to Article 5 stand. We stand FULLY BEHIND them."

CARNEY VISITS CHINA TO STRENGTHEN TRADE RELATIONSHIPS

Mark Carney's visit to China comes after years of tensions in relations with China. Carney wanted to reduce Canada's reliance on the United States amid the difficulties that Canada has been having with the US.

Although Canada sends about 70 percent of its exports to the US, as Carney was leaving for Beijing, Trump told reporters that the US doesn't need Canadian products. Comments like this underscore the need to diversify Canada's exports away from the US. Carney's comment that the partnerships between the two countries are set for the "new world order" was taken by some to mean that the days of a US-led world order will soon be over.

China and Canada also agreed to allow up to 49,000 Chinese electric vehicles into the Canadian market in exchange for lowering Chinese tariffs on Canadian canola. Although welcomed by some senior Canadian politicians, others wanted an explanation from Carney on how he went from saying China was Canada's biggest security threat before the election to engaging in a strategic partnership with China.

Carney also outlined red lines for Canada, including concerns about human rights and interference in Canadian elections. But Carney also said: "We take the world as it is – not as we wish it to be."

CARNEY'S SPEECH AT THE WORLD ECONOMIC FORUM IN DAVOS.

On January 20th, Prime Minister Carney delivered a speech at the World Economic Forum in Davos, Switzerland, which was well received both at home and abroad. He suggested that the U.S.-led, rules-based international order was over. He also urged the middle powers, such as Canada, to form new alliances. He emphasized reliance on unpredictable superpowers and advocated a value-based realism focused on economic diversification and strategic partnerships. He highlighted Canada's strengths, including energy, natural resources, and critical minerals. This speech was also perceived as a shift in foreign policy, with a focus on not relying on the US.

TRUMP BLASTS CARNEY AFTER DAVOS SPEECH

Carney, in his Davos speech, called out the US, a traditional ally of Canada, for a rupture of the role-based order. Following this, Trump responded in his own Davos speech, saying that Canada exists because of the United States and telling Carney to remember this next time he makes a statement. A few days later, Trump threatened to impose a 100 per cent tariff on Canadian goods if Canada made a deal with China. Although Trump has called Canada's agreement with China "a good thing" just a few days ago. Trump also called Carney the governor. Trump suggested that Canada needed to be more grateful.

TRUMP WITHDRAWS CANADA'S INVITATION FOR THE BOARD OF PEACE.

Donald Trump decided to withdraw Canada's invitation to the Board of Peace in January 2026. This may be a reaction to Carney's criticism of US foreign policy and

Canada's hesitation to join and refusal to pay a $1 billion to be a partner in Gaza's reconstruction.

U.S. TREASURY SECRETARY SCOTT BESSENT STATEMENT ABOUT CARNEY

U.S. Treasury Secretary Scott Bessent said he would encourage Prime Minister Carney to do what he thinks is best for the Canadian people, not his own virtue-signalling, because we do have a USMCA negotiation coming up," Bessent further said, Carney rose to power on an anti-American, anti-Trump message, and that's not a great place to be when you're negotiating with an economy that is multiples larger than you are and your biggest trading partner. Bessent also commented, "I would not pick a fight going into USMCA to score some cheap political points."

CARNEY'S DEVOS SPEECH AND HIS STATEMENTS ON VENEZUELA

Carney focused on the rupture of the rule-based international order and the rule of law in his speech at the World Economic Forum in Davos. However, he had failed to condemn Trump's kidnapping of the President of Venezuela, which was against international law. Many found his actions at odds with his words.

POILIEVRE WON LEADERSHIP REVIEW

On January 30, Poilievre won a leadership review with 87% approval from Conservative Party delegates. Although he maintained strong support among his Conservative base through record fundraising, national polling showed that 62% of non-Conservatives had a negative opinion of him after the loss in the 2025 election.

CARNEY REMOVED ISLAMOPHOBIA AND HOLOCAUST REMEMBRANCE REPRESENTATIVES

In February, Carney's government eliminated the position of the Special Representative on Combating Islamophobia, which was created in 2023 under Justin Trudeau. The Envoy position for Holocaust Remembrance was also dissolved. The government decided to create a new Advisory Council on Rights, Equality and Inclusion. This decision created disappointment in the racial minorities, already facing discrimination and hatred.

ALBERTA PREMIER DANIELLE SMITH BLAMED IMMIGRANTS FOR SOCIAL SERVICES CRISES IN ALBERTA

In February 2026, Alberta Premier Danielle Smith blamed the influx of new immigrants, driven by the federal government's disastrous policies, for the strain on the provincial education and healthcare systems. She also held new immigrants responsible for a billion-dollar deficit in the Alberta budget. She said population growth has made classrooms and hospitals overcrowded, and she announced a referendum in Alberta for October 2026 to restrict social programs, education, and healthcare for non-permanent residents. This was strongly criticized, as just a few years earlier, she had demanded that the federal government send more immigrants to Alberta.

CANADIAN POLL ABOUT THE US AND TRUMP

In one of Politico's polls, in Canada and some European countries, most respondents said the U.S. no longer reflects their values. They said that the US exacerbates conflict rather than solving it. About 58% consider the US not a reliable ally of Canada. Trump's threats to Canada played a major role in changing public opinion. Almost 57% of Canadians now say they'd rather depend on China than Trump's America.

TRUMP KEEPS ON CALLING "GOVERNOR CARNEY"

On March 10, Trump referred to Carney as the "future Governor of Canada" in his social media post on Truth Social in reference to working with U.S. governors to "save The Great Lakes from the rather violent and destructive Asian Carp." In January, Trump also commented on his Truth Social post about China making a deal with Canada, "If Governor Carney thinks he is going to make Canada a 'Drop Off Port' for China to send goods and products into the United States, he is sorely mistaken." Carney, in his response, said he won't "comment on every tweet and he can handle it.

CARNEY VISITED INDIA DESPITE INDIA'S INVOLVEMENT IN SUPPORTING CRIMINAL GANGS IN CANADA

In March 2026, Carney visited India to boost bilateral trade and economic cooperation and to reset relations affected by previous diplomatic tensions. There were agreements on the uranium deal, a new comprehensive economic partnership agreement, and memoranda covering AI, critical minerals, and agriculture. There was a focus on a stronger, more collaborative relationship between the two countries.

THE SIKH COMMUNITY AND HUMAN RIGHTS GROUPS PROTEST CARNEY'S INDIA VISIT

Since Canadian Intelligence Agencies had reported in 2025 about the involvement of the Indian government in the murder of a Sikh Community Leader, Hardeep Singh Nijjar, in BC, the Sikh community protested the visit of Carney to India. Also, due to human rights violations and persecution of Muslims, Christians, Buddhists in India, and discriminatory polices of the

BJP government of Modi against minorities, many human rights activists opposed the visit of Carney to India.

THE CARNEY GOVERNMENT DECLINES INDIA'S INVOLVEMENT IN CRIMINAL ACTIVITIES IN CANADA.

Although Former Prime Minister Justin Trudeau announced in October 2024 in the House of Commons about the involvement of India in the murder of a Canadian citizen, Hardeep Singh Nijjar, on Canadian soil, the Carney government officials claimed before Carney's visit to India that there was no Indian interference in Canada.

RCPM INVESTIGATIONS ABOUT INDIA'S INVOLVEMENT IN THE MURDER OF A SIKH CANADIAN

In October 2024, the Royal Canadian Mounted Police (RCMP) made allegations linking the agents of the Government of India to serious criminal activities against Canadian citizens, particularly within the South Asian and Sikh community. The RCMP alleged that Indian diplomats and consular officials used organized crime groups, specifically the Lawrence Bishnoi gang, to carry out violent acts in Canada, including the murder of Sikh community leader Hardeep Singh Nijjar, who was killed in Surrey, B.C., in June 2023. Agents of the Indian government were also involved in intimidation, shootings, and extortions, and many Canadians were warned by the RCMP that they were potential targets of threats by Indian agents.

After claims by the Carney government that India was not involved in criminal activities in Canada, an RCMP acknowledgement emerged regarding ongoing investigations into the involvement of Indian government agents. Canadian media outlets had published reports about the link between the assassination of Hardeep Singh Nijjar and the Indian government.

LIBERAL MPS DHALIWAL AND BAINS REJECT THE LIBERAL GOVERNMENT'S CLAIM ABOUT THE INVOLVEMENT OF INDIA IN CRIMES IN CANADA

Sukh Dhaliwal, Liberal MP from Surrey-Newton riding, where people have been victims of suspected Indian government operations, rejected the Liberal government's official statement that the Indian government is not involved in criminal activities in Canada. He said, "I strongly condemn these statements made by this official because he's not in touch with the realities on the ground," He also remarked "I'm dealing with the community and the victims almost on a regular basis. And this is totally irresponsible," he also said "People across Canada, they are all coming to me and telling me the same thing, that this is still continuing." MP Dhaliwal said he believes he was himself targeted by Indian foreign interference. But he said victims are reluctant to speak out because they fear for their families in India. He said, "It's very hard for them to come out and publicly speak. And basically, they are pressured, either diplomatically or forcibly."

Another Liberal MP, Parm Bains, issued a similar statement rejecting the government official's "attempt to downplay India's involvement in transnational repression and violent criminal activity in Canada." He said, Such a claim undermines public safety, dismisses the tireless work of our security agencies, contradicts findings from the NSIA, RCMP, and CSIS, and raises serious concerns about the official's continued suitability for their role."

CRITICISM OF CARNEY'S GOVERNMENT FOR PUTTING TRADE OVER LIVES AND THE SAFETY OF CANADIANS.

The Carney government was criticized for putting trade over the safety and lives of Canadians, and there were calls for the resignation of the Minister of Foreign Affairs.

RCMP WARNED SIKH LEADER IN BC

Vancouver police have warned Moninder Singh, President of Sikh Federation of Canada, of a threat to his life and the lives of his wife and two children in February 2026, just before Carney's visit to India. Singh suspects these threats are linked to the Indian government due to his advocacy against the oppression of Sikhs in India. Because of these threats, he cannot take his children to public places.

SIKH COMMUNITY MEMBERS DEMAND CLOSURE OF INDIAN CONSULATE IN VANCOUVER

Sikh Community members and the Sikhs for Justice (SFJ) organization demanded the closure of the Indian consulate in Vancouver. A siege of the consulate office was organized by the protesters on the anniversary of Hardeep Singh Nijjar's killing. They believe the consulate officials use their position to spy on and threaten the innocent members of the Sikh community.

CARNEY CRITICIZED FOR HIS SUPPORT OF THE US ATTACK ON IRAN

Carney was in Australia on his Indo-Pacific trip when the US attacked Iran in the middle of negotiations on Iran's pursuit of nuclear technology. Although he called on both parties to de-escalate, he said that while he supports the US in these strikes, he takes that position "with regret". He said that Canada has "long supported the imperative of neutralizing this grave global threat". His statement was widely criticized for his support for the breach of International Law by the US attack on Iran. People again referred to his speech in Davos as nothing more than empty words.

POILIEVRE SUPPORTS THE US ATTACK ON IRAN

Poilievre expressed his support for the attack by the US on Iran and said the US and its allies should take action against Iran. He backed military actions aimed against the Iranian regime. This was widely criticized since an attack on a school in Iran killed more than 150 schoolgirls. Many people called it warmongering and spoke out against the breach of international law.

CANADIANS CONDEMN THE US ATTACK ON IRAN

Most Canadians and practitioners of International Law condemned the US attack on Iran as a clear violation of international law. Foreign Minister of Oman, the country hosting negotiations between Iran and the US, during an interview, said that Iran had agreed to discontinue its nuclear program, and the deal was very close to being finalized when the US attacked Iran. Trump used negotiations as a shield, which damaged the US's credibility. Canadians widely criticized the Conservative Party leader's statement endorsing an attack on Iran and called out Carney on his flip-flop position on this issue. Carney's initial statement supporting the attack on Iran generated a lot of criticism since, in his Devos speech in January, Carney said Canada would remain "principled in our commitment to fundamental values," including "the prohibition of the use of force except when consistent with the UN Charter."

LIBERAL MP FROM VICTORIA REJECTS CARNEY'S SUPPORT FOR THE US ATTACK ON IRAN

Liberal MP Will Greaves commented after Carney's statement on the US attack on Iran, "Canada cannot endorse the unilateral and illegal use of military force, the killing of civilians or the kidnapping and assassination of foreign heads of government while also insisting that our sovereignty, our rights and our independence must be respected." MP Greaves was a professor of international relations at the University of Victoria before being elected MP in 2025.

NDP MP FLOOR CROSSED THE FLOOR TO JOIN THE LIBERALS

Lori Idlout, MP from Nunavut, crossed the floor to join the Liberals. This left the NDP with only six seats and will help Carney secure a majority government if the Liberals win the By-elections in April.

CARNEY LIBERALS VOTE DOWN BILL C-233, "NO MORE LOOPHOLES BILL."

On March 11, NDP MP Jenny Kwan tabled a Private Member's Bill in the House of Commons to close loopholes in Canada's arms export laws that allow

Canadian-made weapons to go into the hands of governments involved in war crimes.

If passed, this bill would have strengthened Canada's compliance with the Arms Trade Treaty (ATT). Although Canada joined the treaty in 2019, exports to the United States were exempt. The bill was to ensure that Canadian-made weapons cannot be used to fuel war, repression, or attacks on civilians, according to MP Jenny Kwan. All NDP MPs and most Muslim MPs voted in favour of this Bill, except Muslim MP Shafqat Ali from Brampton and Yasir Naqvi from Ottawa. This Bill was voted down.

CARNEY ANNOUNCES CANADA WILL NOT JOIN IRAQ WAR

Carney said in the House of Commons that Canada is not involved in the U.S.-Iran war and "will never participate in it." Parliamentarians have been asking the Prime Minister about Canada's position on the war in Iran. Bloc Québécois Leader Yves-François Blanchet raised the war in Iran and called on Carney to share his vision for the Middle East with parliamentarians. Carney said, "Canada's stance is clear. Canada supports the necessity to prevent Iran's nuclear program and the export of terrorism." Carney said he is in contact with the G7 leaders, and they said they will find a common stance on de-escalation in Iran.

THE CANADIAN GOVERNMENT PASSED THE "ANTI-HATE BILL

In March 2026, the Liberal government passed C-9, an anti-hate bill with the support of the Bloc Québécois. Conservatives and the NDP voted against the legislation. This bill proposes new Criminal Code offences, making it a crime to intentionally promote hatred against identifiable groups in public using certain hate or terrorism-related symbols. Faith-based communities, religious groups, racial minorities and the Canadian Civil Liberties Association argued that this legislation could criminalize peaceful protest.

CANADA REACHED 2% NATO'S DEFENCE SPENDING

Canada crossed the threshold of meeting NATO's defence spending benchmark of two per cent of GDP for the first time since the late 1980s. The Canadian government injected more than $9 billion into the Department of National Defence's budget in June, increasing the defence expenditures to more than $61 billion. Trump has repeatedly criticized Canada for failing to fulfill its commitment to NATO. Canada's defence spending is still in the lower range with Spain and Belgium.

REPORTS OF RCMP SPYING ON INDIGENOUS PEOPLE

In March 2026, CBC investigations reported that the RCMP was spying on the members of

National Indian Brotherhood, predecessor of the Assembly of First Nations, while Secwépemc leader George Manuel was the national chief. RCMP was recording his conversations and activities, and he was under physical and electronic surveillance while he organized resistance to the Canadian government's plan to assimilate Indigenous people in the 1960s. RCMP admitted that it was due to Manuel's anti-government feelings. RCMP infiltrated to curb the political activism of the Indigenous organizations in the 1970s through surveillance and penetrating informants.

NDP ELECTED A NEW LEADER

On March 29, NDP members elected Avi Lewis as their new leader after Jagmeet Singh resigned. He received 56% of the votes on the first ballot. He ran his campaign as an "anti-capitalist movement" and promised a national cap on rent, a wealth tax on the 1 per cent of highest income earners, and public funding for groceries and telecoms.

CHAPTER 11

Reflection

This book delves into the pressing issue of increasing political polarization in Canada. It examines how historical, social, and ideological conflicts since Canada's inception have shaped the nation's political landscape. Unity, a cornerstone of any thriving democracy, is at risk in Canada as polarization deepens, mirroring trends observed in its southern neighbour, the United States.

Canada's political division has long been rooted in its history, with tensions between French and English, Indigenous and Immigrant communities, and regional disparities such as Eastern versus Western Canada. Over the past two decades, these divisions have widened, exacerbated by ideological shifts, debates on issues like sexual orientation, gun control, climate change, and economic disparity. Political leaders, instead of bridging gaps, have often exploited these divides for personal or party gains, further eroding our national unity.

The book also highlights the profound impact of Donald J. Trump's presidency on Canada. The rise of Trumpism, characterized by divisive rhetoric and political tribalism, has influenced Canadian society in various ways. From emboldened extremist groups to heightened polarization, the Trump era has caused a lasting imprint on Canada's political and social dynamics. Events like the January 6th Capitol Hill riots in the US serve as cautionary tales of how unchecked division can threaten democracy.

In addition to affecting the social fabric of Canadian society, Trump-era U.S. tariffs have significantly affected Canada's economic growth. Increasing unemployment and uncertainty in business markets have led to decreased investments. Daily changes in Donald Trump's statements, along with fluctuating tariffs on steel, aluminum, and the auto industry, have led to supply chain disruptions. Canada is relying only on CUSMA clauses for exemptions to prevent further harm and is being forced to do so to mitigate any damage.

Trump's threat of a 25% across-the-board tariff will reduce the demand for Canadian exports. Tariffs have impacted the construction sector, resulting in layoffs and reduced employment in sectors that depend upon the US exports. Canada did announce retaliatory tariffs on American imports, but later postponed them to promote negotiations. Many Canadians business firms utilize CUSMA to avoid tariffs. They focus on buying Canadian or exploring alternatives to the US suppliers. Such uncertainty and reduced exports would contribute to a depreciation of the Canadian currency. Long-term consequences of Trump's tariffs include higher inflation, slowed economic growth, and higher prices of goods. Canada needs to diversify its economy to have less reliance on the US, its main trading partner.

Through an exploration of Canada's political history, readers are challenged to reflect on the following crucial questions:

> ➢ Can Canadian political parties prioritize problem-solving over partisan rivalry?

> ➢ Should transparency, accountability, and unity be enforced beyond mere ideals?

> ➢ How can Canadian institutions safeguard against political extremism and foreign interference?

> ➢ Are our current democratic processes robust enough to withstand the pressures of polarization?

There are consequences of unchecked polarization, including weakened trust in democratic institutions, delays in legislative processes, and increased risks of intolerance, discrimination, and social unrest. Is there a need to urge politicians to act as role models and reject extremist rhetoric, while calling for stricter measures to prevent divisive figures from undermining Canada's democracy?

This book is not about assigning blame but about encouraging fellow Canadians to critically assess our political system, demand accountability from leaders, and strive for a more united and inclusive society. It serves as both a reflection on Canada's past and a call to action to preserve its democratic values, inclusion and unity in the face of growing division.

References

Abedi, M. (2019). "Lack of Federal Response to Quebec's Bill 21 'Very Disappointing': Advocates," *Global News.* https://globalnews.ca/news/5408867/quebec-bill-21-federal-response/

Abedi, M. (2020). "A Look at Islamophobia in Canada, 3 Years After the Quebec Mosque Shooting," *Global News.* https://globalnews.ca/news/6472549/muslim-canadians-islamophobia-quebec-city-shooting/

Abramowitz, Alan I.; Saunders, Kyle L. (27 March 2008). "Is Polarization a Myth?". The Journal of Politics. 70 (2): 542.

Adams, Michael (September 26, 2017). Could It Happen Here? Canada in the Age of Trump and Brexit. Simon and Schuster.

Aiello, R. (2021). O'Toole Defends Removing Senator Calling for Leadership Vote as 'Necessary' for Conservative Unity. CTV News. https://www.ctvnews.ca/politics/o-toole-defends-removing-senator-calling-for-leadership-vote-as-necessary-for-conservative-unity-1.5669825Aiello,

Anaya, James. (2014). "Report of the Special Rapporteur on the rights of Indigenous peoples." United Nations General Assembly Human Rights Council. 2014. pp. 1-26. http://unsr.jamesanaya.org/docs/countries/2014-report-canada-a-hrc-27-52-add-2-en-auversion.pdf

Archibald, C. ; Lambert, M. (2013). "Parti Québécois". *The Canadian Encyclopedia.* https://www.thecanadianencyclopedia.ca/en/article/ parti-quebecois

Arugay, Slater, Aires, Dan (2019). "Polarizing Figures: Executive Power and Institutional Conflict in Asian Democracies". American Behavioral Scientist. 62: 92–106.

Aziz, S. & Boutilier, A. (2021). Erin O'Toole Removes Conservative Senator who Launched Leadership Review Petition. Global News.

Bafumi, Joseph; Shapiro, Robert Y. (27 January 2009). "A New Partisan Voter" (PDF). The Journal of Politics. 71 (1): 1.

Baldassarri, Delia; Gelman, Andrew (2008). "Partisans without Constraint: Political Polarization and Trends in American Public Opinion". *American Journal of Sociology.* 114 (2): 408–446.

Barber, J. (2015). Canada's Conservatives Vow to Create 'Barbaric Cultural Practices' Hotline. The Guardian.

Beal, B., & Macleod, R. (2006). North-West Rebellion. In The Canadian Encyclopedia.

Beeby, D. (2013). Gold-Embossed Business Cards Created for Clement, Hawn Against Rules: Documents. Toronto Star. https://www.thestar.com/news/canada/2013/12/08/ goldembossed_business_cards_created_for_clemen t_hawn_against_rules_documents.html

Beeby, D. (2014). "Foreign-aid charities join together
    to challenge Canada Revenue Agency audits"
    Toronto Star.
    https://www.thestar.com/news/canada/2014/08/10/f
    oreignaid_charities_join_together_to_challenge_ca
    nada_revenue_agency_audits.html

Beers, D. (2012). "Minister Moore's Sucker Punch to
    the CBC" The Tyee.
    https://thetyee.ca/Mediacheck/2012/03/30/CBC-
    Budget-Cuts/

Beers, D.; Tee Staff and Contributors. (2015). "Harper,
    Serial Abuser of Power: The Evidence Compiled."
    https://thetyee.ca/Opinion/2015/08/10/Harper-
    Abuses-of-Power-Final/

Belon, M. (2014). Tory MP Paul Calandra Ignores
    Questions About Iraq. Talks About Israel Instead.
    HuffPost. Retrieved from
    https://www.huffingtonpost.ca/2014/09/23/paul-
    calandra-iraq-mulcair-scheer-
    neutrality_n_5870714.html

Benkler, Yochai (2018). Network Propaganda:
    Manipulation, Disinformation, and Radicalization
    in American Politics. Oxford Scholarship Online

Berry, D. (2020). "Canadian Multiculturalism Act,"
    The Canadian Encyclopedia.
    https://thecanadianencyclopedia.ca/en/article/canad
    ian-multiculturalism-act

Berthiaume, L. (2013). "Government accused of
    unfairly barring MPs from visiting military bases."
    Ottawa Citizen.

https://ottawacitizen.com/news/politics/government
-accused-of-unfairly-barring-mps-from-visiting-
military-bases

Bir, Surbhi (October 29, 2020). "Trump vs. Biden –
how does the U.S election impact Canada?".
Ryerson University.

Blake, R. B. (2007). Transforming the Nation: Canada
and Brian Mulroney. Montreal and Kingston:
McGill-Queen's University Press. p. 456.

Blanchfield, M. (2010). "Documents expose Harper's
obsession with control." Toronto Star.
https://www.thestar.com/news/canada/2010/06/06/
documents_expose_harpers_obsession_with_contr
ol.html

Blinch, R. (2014). "Harper Is Willing and Able to
Keep Canada Under Surveillance" Huffington
Post. https://www.huffingtonpost.ca/russ-
blinch/harper-surveillance-bill_b_5395404.html

Blyth, Mark (November 15, 2016). "Global Trumpism:
Why Trump's Victory was 30 Years in the Making
and Why It Won't Stop Here". Foreign Affairs.

Boessenkool, Ken (January 8, 2021). "Enough is
enough with Trumpism". The Line.

Bothwell, R. (2012). Jean Chrétien. The Canadian
Encyclopedia.

Boutiller, A. (2014). "Pierre Poilievre attacks head of
Elections Canada" Toronto Star.
https://www.thestar.com/news/canada/2014/04/08/

conservative_minister_launches_personal_attack_o
n_elections_chief.html

Boynton, S.; Gangdev, S. (2019). "B.C. candidate
expelled from PPC asks Maxime Bernier to
denounce racism". Global News.
https://globalnews.ca/news/5897441/bc-ppc-
candidate-expelled/

Brennan, R. (2012). "John Baird announces plan to
close Rights and Democracy group" Toronto Star.
https://www.thestar.com/news/canada/2012/04/03/j
ohn_baird_announces_plans_to_close_rights_and_
democracy_group.html

Brewster, M. (2011). "Bureaucrats who violated
veteran's privacy get 'slap on the wrist'" The
Globe and Mail.
https://www.theglobeandmail.com/news/politics/bu
reaucrats-who-violated-veterans-privacy-get-slap-
on-the-wrist/article569859/

Brewster, M. (2015). "Harper's Office Removes '24
Seven' Videos That May Show Soldiers' Faces."
Huffington Post.
https://www.huffingtonpost.ca/2015/05/05/pmo-
removes-videos-from-
o_n_7211274.html?guccounter=1

Bryden, J; Rennie, S. (2012). "Opposition parties
slam election dirty tricks campaign linked to
Tories" CBC News. 2012.
https://globalnews.ca/news/215052/opposition-
parties-slam-election-dirty-tricks-campaign-linked-
to-tories-2/

Buckner, P. A. (2013). Rebellions of 1837–38. The Canadian Encyclopedia. https://www.thecanadianencyclopedia.ca/en/article/rebellions-of-1837.

Bumsted, J.M. (2006). "Red River Rebellion". The Canadian Encyclopedia. https://www.thecanadianencyclopedia.ca/en/article/red-river-rebellion

Burke, A. (2020). Liberal MP Out of Caucus After Employing Sister for Years Using Public Funds. CBC News. https://www.cbc.ca/news/politics/yasmin-ratansi-liberal-mp-quits-hired-sister-1.5795407

Butts, E. (2006). "North-West Mounted Police". The Canadian Encyclopedia, https://www.thecanadianencyclopedia.ca/en/article/north-west-mounted-police. Accessed 21 May 2021.

Campion-Smith, B. (2013). "Labrador MP Peter Penashue quits Conservative cabinet over 'ineligible' donations" Toronto Star. https://www.thestar.com/news/canada/2013/03/14/labrador_mp_peter_penashue_quits_stephen_harper_cabinet_over_ineligible_donations.html

Campion-Smith, B. (2013). Canada Won't Fund Abortion in Cases of War Rape. Toronto Star. https://www.thestar.com/news/canada/2013/10/04/canada_expands_nofundingforabortion_development_policy.html

Carbert, M. (2019). Trudeau No-Show Leads to Cancellation of Munk Debate on Foreign Policy. The Globe and Mail. https://www.theglobeandmail.com/politics/article-trudeau-no-show-leads-to-cancellation-of-munk-debate-on-foreign-policy/

Careless, J. (2006). Province of Canada (1841-67). In The Canadian Encyclopedia. https://www.thecanadianencyclopedia.ca/en/article/province-of-canada-1841-67

Carmines, E. G.; Ensley, M.J.; Wagner, M.W. (23 October 2012). "Who Fits the Left–Right Divide? Partisan Polarization in the American Electorate". American Behavioral Scientist. 56 (12): 1631–1653. doi:10.1177/0002764212463353

Carothers, T. and O'Donohue, A. (2019). Democracies Divided: the Global Challenge of Political Polarization. Brookings Institution Press.

CBC News. (2007). Mulroney Tried to Cover up Cash Payments he Received in Hotel Rooms: Schreiber. CBC News. https://www.cbc.ca/news/canada/mulroney-tried-to-cover-up-cash-payments-he-received-in-hotel-rooms-schreiber-1.648379

CBC news. (2009). Mulroney-Schreiber Inquiry Steers Clear of 'Airbus Affair' on First Day. CBC News. https://www.cbc.ca/news/canada/mulroney-schreiber-inquiry-steers-clear-of-airbus-affair-on-first-day-1.858831

CBC News. (2014). Leona Aglukkaq Admits Reading Newspaper Was a 'Bad Idea' During Question Period. CBC News. https://www.cbc.ca/news/politics/leona-aglukkaq-admits-reading-newspaper-was-a-bad-idea-during-question-period-1.2859631

CBC News. (2015). Jerry Bance, Conservative Caught Peeing in Mug, No Longer Candidate, Party Says. CBC News. https://www.cbc.ca/news/politics/jerry-bance-marketplace-1.3217797

CBC News. (2016). A Chronology of the Senate Expenses Scandal. CBC News. https://www.cbc.ca/news/politics/senate-expense-scandal-timeline-1.3677457

CBC News. (2020). "The WE Charity Controversy Explained," CBC News. https://www.cbc.ca/news/canada/we-charity-student-grant-justin-trudeau-testimony-1.5666676

CBC Radio. (2015). Pork-A-Palooza: the Pre-Election Spending Rush by Conservative MPs. CBC News. https://www.cbc.ca/radio/asithappens/as-it-happens-friday-edition-1.3175719/pork-a-palooza-the-pre-election-spending-rush-by-conservative-mps-1.3176207

Chase, S. (2012). "Harper government stonewalled detainee probe, watchdog concludes." The Globe and Mail. https://www.theglobeandmail.com/news/politics/harper-government-stonewalled-detainee-probe-watchdog-concludes/article4374184/

Cheadle, B. (2012). "Parliamentary Budget Office Has Gone Too Far: John Baird." Huffington Post. https://www.huffingtonpost.ca/2012/06/19/parliam entary-budget-office_n_1610288.html

Cheadle, B. (2014). "Auditor general: 'Gross mismanagement' in files handled by integrity commissioner." Toronto Star. https://www.thestar.com/news/canada/2014/04/15/ auditor_general_gross_mismanagement_in_files_h andled_by_integrity_commissioner.html

Cheadle, B. (2015). Long-Gun Registry Data Destroyed by RCMP on Tories' Urging, PM Says. Toronto Star. Retrieved from https://www.thestar.com/news/canada/2015/06/16/l ong-gun-registry-date-destroyed-by-rcmp-on-tories-urging.html

Chedale, B. (2015). "Omnibus budget bill rewrites history to clear RCMP of potential criminal charges." Toronto City News. https://toronto.citynews.ca/2015/05/13/omnibus-budget-bill-rewrites-history-to-clear-rcmp-of-potential-criminal-charges/

Cholbi, I. (2019). The Positives of Political Polarization. Berkeley Political Review. Retrieved from https://bpr.berkeley.edu/2019/04/13/the-positives-of-political-polarization/

Claassen, R.L.; Highton, B. (9 September 2008). "Policy Polarization among Party Elites and the Significance of Political Awareness in the Mass Public". Political Research Quarterly. 62 (3): 538–551.

Clark, C. (2013). John Baird Says Holidays at Official Residences Abroad were Favours from Friends. The Globe and Mail. Retrieved from https://www.theglobeandmail.com/news/politics/john-baird-says-holidays-at-official-residences-abroad-were-favours-from-friends/article12727490/

Cobb, C. (2015). "Harper, the message and Canadian democracy" Ottawa Citizen. https://ottawacitizen.com/news/local-news/harper-the-message-and-canadian-democracy

Conacher, D. (2010). "Prorogation and the right to know." Toronto Star.

Conservation Council of New Brunswick (n.d). "TransCanada's Energy East Pipeline: What You Need to Know," *Conservation Council of New Brunswick*. https://www.conservationcouncil.ca/en/our-programs/climate-and-energy/energy-east-pipeline-what-you-need-to-know/#wrap

Coyne, A. (2013). "Stephen Harper's official version of events regarding Mike Duffy scandal strains credulity". National Post. https://nationalpost.com/opinion/stephen-harpers-official-version-of-events-regarding-mike-duffy-scandal-strains-credulity

Crabb, Josh (January 8, 2021). "Manitoba MP faces questions over MAGA hat photo". Winnipeg. CTV News Winnipeg (CKY-DT)

CTV News Staff. (2014). Mounties Formally Charge Harb, Brazeau. CTV News. https://www.ctvnews.ca/politics/mounties-formally-charge-harb-brazeau-1.1669624

Curry, B. (2015). "Poilievre paid public servants overtime to help film promotional video." The Globe and Mail. . https://www.theglobeandmail.com/news/politics/poilievre-paid-public-servants-overtime-to-help-film-promotional-video/article24448233/

Curry, B. (2015). Ethics Report Finds Tory Minister Diane Finley Broke Conflict-Of-Interest Rules. The Globe and Mail. Retrieved from https://www.theglobeandmail.com/news/politics/conservative-minister-finley-breached-conflict-of-interest-rules-watchdog-says/article23385863/

Curry, B.; Hannay, C. (2015). "Government favours infrastructure projects to Conservative ridings" The Globe and Mail. https://www.theglobeandmail.com/news/politics/government-favours-infrastructure-projects-to-conservative-ridings/article25492064/

Darity, William A. (2009), "Economic theory and racial economic inequality", in Dodson, Howard; Palmer, Colin A. (eds.), The Black condition, East Lansing, Michigan: Michigan State University Press, pp. 1–43.

Davey, Hampton (1 August 1972). "Polarization and Consensus in Indian Party Politics". Asian Survey. 12 (8): 701–716.

De Souza, M. (2013). "Harper government cutting more than $100 million related to protection of water." Canada.com. https://o.canada.com/news/harper-government-cutting-more-than-100-million-related-to-protection-of-water

Deachman, B. (2020). Citizen@175: "I Might as Well give you a Blast to Wake You Up.' Ottawa Citizen. Retrieved from https://ottawacitizen.com/news/local-news/citizen175-i-might-as-well-give-you-a-blast-to-wake-you-up

Delacourt, S. (2011). "Commons Speaker slams 'reprehensible' politics". Toronto Star. https://www.thestar.com/news/canada/2011/12/13/commons_speaker_slams_reprehensible_politics.html

Delacourt, S. (2012). Industry Minister Christian Paradis Caught in Conflict of Interest for Rahim Jaffer Dealings. Toronto Star. https://www.thestar.com/news/canada/2012/03/22/industry_minister_christian_paradis_caught_in_conflict_of_interest_for_rahim_jaffer_dealings.html

Delacourt, Susan (November 8, 2020). "Donald Trump lost, but Trumpism is still thriving. Could it take hold in Canada, too?". Toronto Star.

DeVoretz, D. J & Pivnenko, S. (2007). "The Immigration Triangle: Quebec, Canada and the Rest of the World," *Discussion Paper Series*. http://ftp.iza.org/dp2624.pdf

Do, T. T. (2015). Long-Gun Registry Records Destroyed by RCMP Under 'a Lot of Pressure' from Ontario. CBC News. https://www.cbc.ca/news/politics/long-gun-registry-records-destroyed-by-rcmp-under-a-lot-of-pressure-from-ottawa-1.3113990

Don, M. (2014). "Conservatives copyright changes could cast political chill" CTV News. https://www.ctvnews.ca/ctv-news-channel/power-play/conservative-s-copyright-changes-could-cast-political-chill-1.2047547

Donolo, Peter (August 21, 2020). "Trumpism won't happen in Canada – but not because of our politics". The Globe and Mail.

Donolo, Peter (January 9, 2021). "What will become of Trump's Canadian fan base?". Toronto Star. Toronto, Ontario

Dryden, J. (2020). "Kenney Resists Calls to Fire Speechwriter Who Said Residential Schools were a 'Bogus Genocide Story," CBC News. https://www.cbc.ca/news/canada/calgary/jason-kenney-rachel-notley-gabrielle-lindstrom-paul-bunner-1.5627422

Duhaime, Erik; Apfelbaum, Evan (2017). "Can Information Decrease Political Polarization? Evidence From the U.S. Taxpayer Receipt". Social Psychological and Personality Science. 8 (7): 736.

Editors of the Encyclopaedia Britannica (2020). "Canada Act," Encyclopaedia Britannica.

Retrieved
fromhttps://www.britannica.com/event/Canada-Act

Edsall, T. (2018). What motivates Voters More than Loyalty? Loathing. The New York Times. https://www.nytimes.com/2018/03/01/opinion/negative-partisanship-democrats-republicans.html

Elghawaby, A. & Munir, H. (2017). History of Muslims in Canada Reminds us all of who we are.

Failler, A. (2009). Remembering the Air India Disaster Memorial and Counter Memorial. Review of Education, Pedagogy, and Cultural Studies. 32(2).

Fawcett, Max (January 12, 2021). "Rigged Canadian election? Why Canada's Conservatives can't seem to quit Donald Trump". National Observer.

Fawcett, Max (January 27, 2022). "Anti-vaxxer truck convoy signals insidious spread of Trumpism in Canada". National Observer.

Fekete, J. (2011). 'Rules were broken' over G8/G20 summit spending: Auditor-General" National Post. https://nationalpost.com/news/canada/rules-were-broken-over-g8g20-summit-spending-auditor-general/

Fiorina, Morris P.; Abrams, Samuel J. (1 June 2008). "Political Polarization in the American Public". Annual Review of Political Science. 11 (1): 563–588.

Fisher, Marc (May 16, 2019). "After a two-decade friendship and waves of lavish praise, Trump pardons newspaper magnate Conrad Black". The Washington Post.

Fitzpatrick, M. (2012). Bev Oda Retiring with Pride and No OJ Regrets. CBC News. https://www.cbc.ca/news/politics/bev-oda-retiring-with-pride-and-no-oj-regrets-1.1191636

Foot, R.; Marshall, T. (2019). Canadian Senate Expenses Scandal. The Canadian Encyclopedia. Retrieved from https://www.thecanadianencyclopedia.ca/en/article/canadian-senate-expenses-scandal

Foot. R. (2018). "Canadian Charter of Rights and Freedoms," The Canadian Encyclopedia. Retrieved byhttps://www.thecanadianencyclopedia.ca/en/article/canadian-charter-of-rights-and-freedoms

Fournier, Philippe J. (January 10, 2021). "Canada is not immune to Trumpism". Maclean's.

Fournier, Philippe J. (October 1, 2020). "How much do Canadians dislike Donald Trump? A lot". Maclean's.

Gall, G. (2013). "Québec Referendum (1995)." *The Canadian Encyclopedia.* https://www.thecanadianencyclopedia.ca/en/article/quebec-referendum-1995

Gall, G. L. (2006). "Charlottetown Accord". *The Canadian Encyclopedia.* https://www.thecanadianencyclopedia.ca/en/article/the-charlottetown-accord

Gall, G.L (2006). "Meech Lake Accord," *The Canadian Encyclopedia.* https://www.thecanadianencyclopedia.ca/en/article/meech-lake-accord

Gall, G.L (2006). Meech Lake Accord. *The Canadian Encyclopedia.* https://www.thecanadianencyclopedia.ca/en/article/meech-lake-accord

Galletti, N.; Lemieux, M. (2010). "The dismantling of Canadian democracy promotion, brick by brick" The Globe and Mail. https://www.theglobeandmail.com/opinion/the-dismantling-of-canadian-democracy-promotion-brick-by-brick/article1321638/

Galloway, G. (2007). "Tory whip defends manual on disrupting committee meetings." The Globe and Mail. https://www.theglobeandmail.com/news/national/tory-whip-defends-manual-on-disrupting-committee-meetings/article686094/

Galloway, Gloria. (2011). "Harper government falls in historic Commons showdown." The Globe and Mail. https://www.theglobeandmail.com/news/politics/harper-government-falls-in-historic-commons-showdown/article4181393/

Galston, William A. (2009). "Political Polarization and the U.S. Judiciary". UKMC Law Review. 77 (207)

García-Guadilla, María Pilar; Mallen, Ana (2019-01-01). "Polarization, Participatory Democracy, and

Democratic Erosion in Venezuela's Twenty-First Century Socialism". The Annals of the American Academy of Political and Social Science. 681 (1): 62–77.

Garner, Andrew; Palmer, Harvey (June 2011). "Polarizationand issue consistency over time". Political Behavior. Springer. 33 (2): 225–246.

Gatehouse, J. (2013). "When science goes silent" Maclean's. https://www.macleans.ca/news/canada/when-science-goes-silent/

Gibbs, K.; Houben, A.; Hutchings, J.; Orihel, D.; Moores, A. Trudeau L. V. (2012). "'The Death of Evidence in Canada: Scientists' Own Words" The Tyee. https://thetyee.ca/Opinion/2012/07/16/Death-of-Evidence/

Gilchrist, E. (2014). Right-Wing Charities Escaping CRA Audits: New Reports from Broadbent Institute. The Narwhal. Retrieved from https://thenarwhal.ca/right-wing-charities-escaping-cra-audits-new-report-broadbent-institute/

Gillis, W. (2020). "What led to Dafonte Miller's 'horrific' eye injury? Theriault brothers' trial closes with perjury claims". Toronto Star. https://www.thestar.com/news/gta/2020/01/29/closing-arguments-begin-today-in-trial-of-michael-and-christian-theriault-accused-of-beating-dafonte-miller.html

Gilmore, R. (2020). O'Toole Tells Students Residential Schools Created to 'Provide Education' but Became 'Horrible.' Global News. Retrieved from https://globalnews.ca/news/7524370/otoole-residential-schools-eduction-horrible/

GLASSFORD, L. (1992). The 1935 Election: Going Down with the Ship. In Reaction and Reform: The Politics of the Conservative Party under R.B. Bennett, 1927-1938 (pp. 175-204). Toronto; Buffalo; London: University of Toronto Press. August 25, 2020, http://www.jstor.org/stable/10.3138/j.ctt1vgw9kb.12

Global News Staff. (2018). "Maxime Bernier slams Justin Trudeau's cult of diversity in Twitter rant". Global News. https://globalnews.ca/news/4385065/maxime-bernier-twitter-diversity-justin-trudeau/

Glover, F. (2020). "The Quebec Act, 1774 (Plain-Language Summary)". The Canadian Encyclopedia.

Granatstein, J., & Jones, R. (2006), "Conscription in Canada," The Canadian Encyclopedia. https://www.thecanadianencyclopedia.ca/en/article/conscription

Granatstein, J.J. (2018). "Conscription Divided Canada. It Also Helped Win the First World War," Maclean's. https://www.macleans.ca/news/canada/conscription-divided-canada-it-also-helped-win-the-first-world-war/

Graves, Frank; Smith, Jeff (June 30, 2020). "Northern Populism: Causes and Consequences of the New Ordered Outlook". School of Public Policy. **13**

Grenier, É. (2020). "Most Canadians believe systemic racism exists — but could it affect how they vote?". *CBC News*. https://www.cbc.ca/news/politics/grenier-systemic-racism-election-issue-1.5610244

Gunter, L. (2021). GUNTER: O'Toole Turns Back on Supporters with Carbon Tax Proposal. Edmonton Sun. https://edmontonsun.com/opinion/columnists/gunter-otoole-turns-back-on-supporters-with-carbon-tax-proposal

Hall, A. J. (2006). "Royal Proclamation of 1763". The Canadian Encyclopedia. https://www.thecanadianencyclopedia.ca/en/article/royal-proclamation-of-1763

Harper, T. (2014). "Our unfixed election date: Tim Harper" Toronto Star. https://www.thestar.com/news/canada/2014/04/20/our_unfixed_fixed_election_date_tim_harper.html

Harper, T. (2015). "Senate is merely home to Stephen Harper's puppets: Tim Harper" Toronto Star. 2015. https://www.thestar.com/news/canada/2015/06/26/senate-is-merely-home-to-stephen-harpers-puppets-tim-harper.html

Harris, K. (2016). Judge Clears Mike Duffy of All Charged and Slams Prime Minister's Office Under Harper. CBC News.

https://www.cbc.ca/news/politics/mike-duffy-trial-rulings-fraud-bribery-senate-1.3545846

Harris, S. (2014). Canada Job Grant ads Cost $2.5M for Non-Existent Program. CBC News. https://www.cbc.ca/news/politics/canada-job-grant-ads-cost-2-5m-for-non-existent-program-1.2495196

Hayward, J. (2011). "Tories re-brand government in Stephen Harper's name." The Globe and Mail. 2011. https://www.theglobeandmail.com/news/politics/tories-re-brand-government-in-stephen-harpers-name/article569222/

Hetherington, Marc J. (17 February 2009). "Review Article: Putting Polarization in Perspective". British Journal of Political Science. 39 (2): 413.

Hetherington, Marc J. (17 February 2009). "Review Article: Putting Polarization in Perspective". British Journal of Political Science. 39 (2): 413.

Hildebrandt, A. (2013). Half of First Nations Children Live in Poverty. CBC News. half-of-first-nations-children-live-in-poverty-1.1324232.

Hilderbrandt, A. (2013). Half of First Nations Children Live in Poverty. CBC News. http://www.cbc.ca/news/canada/half-of-first-nations-children-live-in-poverty-1.1324232

Hillmer, N. & Azzi, S. (2007). Paul Martin. The Canadian Encyclopedia. https://thecanadianencyclopedia.ca/index.php/en/article/paul-edgar-philippe-martin

Hillmer, N. (2013). "Brian Mulroney". *The Canadian Encyclopedia.* https://www.thecanadianencyclopedia.ca/en/article/brian-mulroney

History.com editors. (2009). War of 1812. History. https://www.history.com/topics/war-of-1812/war-of-1812#section_2

Hohenberg, Clemm von; Bernhard; Maes, Michael; Pradelski, Bary S.R. (2017-05-25). "Micro influence and macro dynamics of opinions".

Hollander, B.A. (1 March 2008). "Tuning Out or Tuning Elsewhere? Partisanship, Polarization, and Media Migration from 1998 to 2006". Journalism & Mass Communication Quarterly. 85 (1): 23–40.

Howard, V.(2009). Unemployment Relief Camps. In The Canadian Encyclopedia. https://www.thecanadianencyclopedia.ca/en/article/unemployment-relief-camps

https://globalnews.ca/news/8378978/erin-otoole-removes-senator-denise-batters/

https://ottawacitizen.com/news/national/the-gargoyle-harper-tories-unleash-torrent-of-patronage-appointments

https://web.archive.org/web/20140227154800/http://www.pbc-clcc.gc.ca/infocntr/multi-eng.shtml

https://www.thecanadianencyclopedia.ca/en/article/joseph-jacques-jean-chretien

https://www.thecanadianencyclopedia.ca/en/article/north-west-rebellion

https://www.theguardian.com/world/2015/oct/02/canada-conservatives-barbaric-cultural-practices-hotline

https://www.thestar.com/opinion/editorialopinion/2010/01/18/prorogation_and_the_right_to_know.htm

Hudon, R. (2013). "Québec Referendum (1980)". *The Canadian Encyclopedia.* https://www.thecanadianencyclopedia.ca/en/article/quebec-referendum-1980

Hyslop, K. (2012). "Taking on the Feds for Aboriginal Equality" The Tyee. https://thetyee.ca/News/2012/04/20/Aboriginal-Equality/

Ibbitson, J. (2009). "Partisan cheques put Tories in hot water." The Globe and Mail. https://www.theglobeandmail.com/news/politics/partisan-cheques-put-tories-in-hot-water/article4316924/

Ivanov, A. (2019). "Justin Trudeau should have kept his Hands Off SNC-Lavalin," *The Globe and Mail.* https://www.theglobeandmail.com/opinion/editorials/article-justin-trudeau-should-have-kept-his-hands-off-snc-lavalin/

Ivison, J. (2012). John Ivison: How Stephen Harper learned to love the omnibus bill. National Post. https://nationalpost.com/opinion/john-ivison-how-stephen-harper-learned-to-love-omnibus-bills

Ivison, J. (2012). "John Ivison: Criticism by Conservative MP shows depth of unease over omnibus budget bill." National Post. https://nationalpost.com/opinion/john-ivison-criticism-by-conservative-mp-shows-depth-of-unease-over-omnibus-budget-bill

Ivison, J. (2012). "John Ivison: Pierre Poutine called voters in ridings across Ontario — not just Guelph" National Post. http://news.nationalpost.com/full-comment/john-ivison-pierre-poutine-called-voters-in-ridings-across-ontario-not-just-guelph#__federated=1

Ivison, J. (2013). "John Ivison: Tories would be incensed by $548M in partisan ad spending if they weren't the ones doing it" National Post. https://nationalpost.com/opinion/john-ivison-tories-would-be-incensed-by-548m-in-partisan-ad-spending-if-they-werent-the-ones-doing-it

Ivison, J. (2014). "John Ivison: Harper's attack on the Chief Justice qualifies as yet another blindside hit." National Post. https://nationalpost.com/opinion/john-ivison-harpers-attack-on-the-chief-justice-qualifies-as-yet-another-blindside-hit-2

Ivison, J. (2014). "John Ivison: In place of answers over Canada's ISIS mission, we got vaudeville." National Post. 2014. https://nationalpost.com/opinion/john-ivison-in-place-of-answers-over-canadas-isis-mission-we-got-vaudeville

Ivison, J. (2014). Peter MacKay Says Controversial Mother's and Father's Day Emails Written by Female Staffer. National Post. Retrieved from https://nationalpost.com/news/politics/peter-mackay-says-controversial-mothers-and-fathers-day-emails-written-by-female-staffer

James, P. (1998). Rational choice? Crisis bargaining over the meech lake accord. *Conflict Management and Peace Science, 16*(2), 149-184. Retrieved September 1, 2020, http://www.jstor.org/stable/26273507

Jilani, Z. and Smith, J. A. (2019). What is the True Cost of Polarization in America? Greater Good Magazine. https://greatergood.berkeley.edu/article/item/what_is_the_true_cost_of_polarization_in_america

Johnston, Richard (17 December 2008). "Polarized Pluralism in the Canadian Party System: Presidential Address to the Canadian Political Science Association, June 5, 2008". Canadian Journal of Political Science. 41 (4): 815.

Jones, K. (2020). "What's behind Canadian Prime Minister Chretien's business scandal?" World Socialist Website. Retrieved from https://www.wsws.org/en/articles/2001/04/chre-a10.html

Jones, R. (2006). "French Canadian Nationalism". *The Canadian Encyclopedia.* https://www.thecanadianencyclopedia.ca/en/article/french-canadian-nationalism

Joseph, R. (2017). "Why Justin Trudeau's Trip to the Aga Khan Island Matters," *Global News*. Retrieved from https://globalnews.ca/news/3180076/why-justin-trudeaus-trip-to-the-aga-khans-island-matters/

Kaplan, W. (2011). "Stephen Harper's five-question limit." The Globe and Mail. https://www.theglobeandmail.com/opinion/stephen-harpers-five-question-limit/article57973

Kellie Leitch "Trump's win an 'exciting message' that's needed in Canada, says". Toronto Star. November 9, 2016.

Kellie Leitch, the potential future prime minister who wants to bring President-elect Trump's message to Canada. November 9, 2016.

Kennedy, M. (2015). "Tories end gag order on people who attend Stephen Harper's events" Ottawa Citizen. https://ottawacitizen.com/news/politics/tories-end-gag-order-on-people-who-attend-stephen-harpers-events

Kennedy, M.; Mayeda, A. (2011). "Harper forced to explain Conservatives' rally rules after students tossed" Canada.com. http://www.canada.com/news/Harper+forced+explain+Conservatives+rally+rules+after+students+tossed/4562633/story.html

Kent, G. (2017). Industry Still Chafed Five Years After End of Canadian Wheat Board Monopoly. Edmonton Sun.

https://edmontonsun.com/2017/08/05/industry-still-chafed-five-years-after-end-of-canadian-wheat-board-monopoly

Kessler, A.; Thunert, M.; Sharpe, A. (2014). "Sustainable Governance Indicators". Bertelsmann Stiftung. pp. 1-42. http://www.sgi-network.org/docs/2014/country/SGI2014_Canada.pdf

Keung, N. (2015). "Immigration detainee's death sparks calls to lift CBSA's 'shroud of secrecy'." Toronto Star. 2015. https://www.thestar.com/news/immigration/2015/06/19/immigration-detainees-death-sparks-calls-to-lift-cbsas-shroud-of-secrecy.html

Keung, N. (2015). "UN alarmed by Canada's immigration detention." Toronto Star. 2015. https://www.thestar.com/news/immigration/2015/07/23/un-alarmed-by-canadas-immigration-detention.html

Kilian, C. (2012). 'Environmentalists, Other Radical Groups,' Threaten Pipeline: Joe Oliver. The Hook. https://thetyee.ca/Blogs/TheHook/Environment/2012/01/09/Environmentalists_other_radical_groups/

Kilpatrick, S. (2011). "Tony Clement kept auditor in dark on G8 spending, municipal files suggest" The Globe and Mail.

Kilpatrick, S. (2014). Senate Still out $45,000 for Patrick Brazeau's Expense Claims. The Globe and Mail. Retrieved from https://www.theglobeandmail.com/news/politics/se

nate-still-out-45000-for-brazeaus-expense-
claims/article21396455/

Kim, S.J. (2011). Emerging patterns of news media use
across multiple platforms and their political
implications in south korea. Northwestern
University.

Kinsinger, K. (2019). "Quebec's Bill 21 Misapplies
Religious Neutrality Principle," *Policy Options
Politiques*. Retrieved from
https://policyoptions.irpp.org/fr/magazines/may-
2019/quebecs-bill-21-misapplies-religious-
neutrality-principle/

Kwong, M. (2015). Canadian Expats Still Feel 'a Lot
of Bitterness' over Lack of Vote. CBC News.
Retrieved from
https://www.cbc.ca/news/politics/canada-election-
2015-expats-vote-1.3275422

La Raja, R.J.; Wiltse, D.L. (13 December 2011).
"Don't Blame Donors for Ideological Polarization
of Political Parties: Change and Stability Among
Political Contributors, 1972–2008". American
Politics Research. 40 (3): 501–530.

Lang, E. (2019). "The Trudeaus and Western
Alienation," *Policy Options Politiques*.
https://policyoptions.irpp.org/magazines/november
-2019/the-trudeaus-and-western-alienation/

LaPierre, L. (1971). "Quebec: October 1970," The
North American Review, 256(3), 23-33. August
29, 2020, from
http://www.jstor.org/stable/25117224

Lau, A. (2015). Bob Zimmer, Conservative Candidate, Says 'Lack of a Job' Is One Reason for Missing, Murdered Women. HuffPost. https://www.huffingtonpost.ca/2015/10/08/bob-zimmer_n_8261406.html

Laurendeau, P. (2006). Official Languages Act (1969). The Canadian Encyclopedia. Retrieved from https://www.thecanadianencyclopedia.ca/en/article/official-languages-act-1969

Layman, Geoffrey C.; Carsey, Thomas M.; Horowitz, Juliana Menasce (1 June 2006). "Party Polarization in American Politics: Characteristics, Causes, and Consequences". Annual Review of Political Science. 9 (1): 83–110.

Layman, Geoffrey C.; Green, John C. (January 2006). "Wars and rumours of wars: the contexts of cultural conflict in American political behaviour". British Journal of Political Science. Cambridge Journals. 36 (1): 61–89.

LeBas, Adrienne; Munemo, Ngonidzashe (2019-01-01). "Elite Conflict, Compromise, and Enduring Authoritarianism: Polarization in Zimbabwe, 1980–2008". The Annals of the American Academy of Political and Social Science. 681 (1): 209–226.

Leblanc, D. & McArthur, G. (2010). Mulroney-Schreiber Relationship 'Inappropriate,' Probe Finds. The Globe and Mail. https://www.theglobeandmail.com/news/politics/mulroney-schreiber-relationship-inappropriate-probe-finds/article4321310/

Lum, Z. (2021). Trudeau Dumps on Bloc Leader's 'Ridiculous' Innuendos About New Minister. Huffpost. https://www.huffingtonpost.ca/entry/trudeau-bloc-quebecois-omar-alghabra_ca_

Maclean's. (2011). John Baird's Gold Card Causes a Stir. Maclean's. https://www.macleans.ca/general/john-bairds-gold-card-causes-a-stir/

Madwar, S. (2018). Inuit High Arctic Relocations in Canada. In The Canadian Encyclopedia. Retrieved from https://www.thecanadianencyclopedia.ca/en/article/inuit-high-arctic-relocations

Maher, S. (2017). "The Aga khan Trip and a Glimpse into Trudeau's Bad Judgement," *Macleans*. Retrieved from https://www.macleans.ca/politics/ottawa/the-aga-khan-trip-and-a-glimpse-into-trudeaus-bad-judgement/

Maher, S. (2019). Why Won't Maxime Bernier Denounce the Terror Attack in christchurch? Macleans. Retrieved from https://www.macleans.ca/opinion/why-wont-maxime-bernier-denounce-the-terror-attack-in-christchurch/

Maher, S.; McGregor, G. (2012). "Conservatives' 'in-and-out' scandal investigation cost taxpayers $2.3-million". National Post. https://nationalpost.com/news/canada/conservative

s-in-and-out-scandal-investigation-cost-taxpayers-
2-3m

Maloney, R. (2014). "The Trudeau Attack Ads Tories
Don't Want You To See... Online (VIDEO)"
Huffington Post.
https://www.huffingtonpost.ca/2014/03/14/trudeau-
attack-ads-2014-online_n_4965474.html

Mann, Thomas E.; Ornstein, Norman J. (2012). It's
Even Worse Than It Looks: How the American
constitutional system collided with the new politics
of extremism. Basic Books.

Mann, Thomas E.; Ornstein, Norman J. (2012). It's
Even Worse Than It Looks: How the American
constitutional system collided with the new politics
of extremism

Marshall, T. (2013). Oka Crisis. The Canadian
Encyclopedia.
https://www.thecanadianencyclopedia.ca/en/article/
oka-crisis

Martin, L. (2011). "To Push Prisons, Harper Buried
Own Government's Findings" The Tyee.
https://thetyee.ca/News/2011/04/29/HarperPushesP
risons/

Martin, L. (2014). "A star like Jason Kenney should
avoid the gutter" The Globe and Mail.
https://www.theglobeandmail.com/opinion/a-star-
like-kenney-should-avoid-the-
gutter/article21858922/

Martin, L. (2014). "Harper's Legislated Loyalty
Threat." The Tyee.

https://thetyee.ca/Opinion/2014/01/17/Harpers-Legislated-Loyalty-Threat/

Martin, Lawrence (January 6, 2022). "Opinion: The disturbing reality is that millions of Canadians support Trump". The Globe and Mail

Mason, Lilliana (January 2013). "The rise of uncivil agreement: issue versus behavioral polarization in the American electorate". American Behavioral Scientist. Sage. 57 (1): 140–159.

Masters, D., Reciprocity (2013). The Canadian Encyclopedia. Retrieved from https://www.thecanadianencyclopedia.ca/en/article/reciprocity

Matt Galloway (Host), Allan Rock (Guest) (November 6, 2020). "Allan Rock on what the presidential election means for U.S.-Canada relations". The Current. Canadian Broadcasting Corporatio

Matt Galloway (Host), Ken Boessenkool (Guest) (January 13, 2020). "Conservatives must reject Trumpism and address voter anger rather than stoking it, says strategist". The Current. Canadian Broadcasting Corporation.

May, K. (2015). "Parliament lost scrutiny of borrowing in omnibus budget bill." Ottawa Citizen. 2015. http://ottawacitizen.com/news/national/parliament-lost-scrutiny-of-borrowing-in-omnibus-budget-bill

McCarty, Nolan; Poole, Keith T.; Rosenthal, Howard (2006). Polarized America : the dance of ideology and unequal riches. MIT Press. Cambridge, Mass.

McCowy, J. and Somer, M. (2018). Toward a Theory of Pernicious Polarization and How It Harms Democracies: Comparative Evidence and Possible Remedies. 681(1). 234-271.

McGregor, G. (2015). "The Gargoyle - Tories unleash torrent of patronage appointments" Ottawa Citizen.

McParland, K. (2013). "Kelly McParland: Media hits new low, tries to report Prime Minister's speech" National Post. http://news.nationalpost.com/full-comment/kelly-mcparland-no-questions-please-yes-cameras-are-still-ok

Mehta, D. (2014). "Ex-Conservative MP Dean Del Mastro guilty on election charges" Toronto Star. https://www.thestar.com/news/canada/2014/10/31/exconservative_mp_dean_del_mastro_guilty_on_election_charges.html

Mick, H. (2006). "Officer cursed teen before shooting, inquest told". *The Globe and Mail.* https://www.theglobeandmail.com/news/national/officer-cursed-teen-before-shooting-inquest-told/article18165059/

Miller, J. (2012). Residential Schools in Canada. In The Canadian Encyclopedia. Retrieved from https://www.thecanadianencyclopedia.ca/en/article/residential-schools

Miller, J. (2012). Residential Schools in Canada. In The Canadian Encyclopedia. Retrieved from https://www.thecanadianencyclopedia.ca/en/article/residential-schools.

Milloy, J. S. (1999). A National Crime. The Canadian
Government and the Residential School System,
1989 to 1986. The University of Manitoba Press.

Miquelon, D.; Massicotte, L.; McIntosh, A. (2006).
"The Conquest of New France". *The Canadian
Encyclopedia.*
https://www.thecanadianencyclopedia.ca/en/article/
conquest

Montpetit, J. & Shingler, B. (2021). Quebec Superior
Court Upholds Most of Religious Symbols ban, but
English-Language Schools Exempt. CBC News.
https://www.cbc.ca/news/canada/montreal/bill-21-
religious-symbols-ban-quebec-court-ruling-
1.5993431

Montpetit, J. (2019). "Quebec City Mosque Shooting, "
The Canadian Encyclopedia. Retrieved from
https://thecanadianencyclopedia.ca/en/article/quebe
c-city-mosque-shooting

Montpetit, J. (2019). Quebec City Mosque Shooting. In
The Canadian Encyclopedia. Retrieved from
https://www.thecanadianencyclopedia.ca/en/article/
quebec-city-mosque-shooting

Moran, R. (2015). Truth and Reconciliation
Commission. The Canadian Encyclopedia.
Retrieved from
https://www.thecanadianencyclopedia.ca/en/article/
truth-and-reconciliation-commission

Morin, B. (2020). As the RCMP Deny Systemic
Racism, Here's the Real History. The Star.
Retrieved from

https://www.thestar.com/opinion/contributors/2020/06/11/rcmp-deputy-commissioners-words-on-racism-fly-in-face-of-150-years-of-history-and-pain-for-Indigenous-peoples.html

Mulroney, B. (2012). Acid Rain: A case study in Canada-US relations. Policy Options. Retrieved from https://policyoptions.irpp.org/magazines/harpers-foreign-policy/acid-rain-a-case-study-in-canada-us-relations/

Munro, M. (2013). "Information commissioner to investigate 'muzzling' of federal scientists" Canada.com. 2013. https://o.canada.com/news/national/information-commissioner-to-investigate-muzzling-of-federal-scientists

Murphy, J. (2019). "How Damaging is Blackface Scandal to Trudeau?" *BBC News*. https://www.bbc.com/news/world-us-canada-49760160

Murphy, J. (2020). "WE Charity Scandal- A Simple Guide to the New Crisis for Trudeau," *BBC News*. https://www.bbc.com/news/world-us-canada-53494560

N.n, (2016). "Women's Suffrage in Manitoba (2016)," The Canadian Encyclopedia. Retrieved from https://www.thecanadianencyclopedia.ca/en/article/womens-suffrage-in-manitoba

N.n. (2005). Transboundary Air: Canada-US Air Quality Agreement. Canada, Environment, and

Climate Change. Retrieved from
https://www.canada.ca/en/environment-climate-
change/services/air-
pollution/issues/transboundary/canada-united-
states-air-quality-agreement.html

N.n. (2006). "Harper on defensive over media ban on
return of dead soldiers" CBC News.
https://www.cbc.ca/news/canada/harper-on-
defensive-over-media-ban-on-return-of-dead-
soldiers-1.598979

N.n. (2007). "Bains 'baffled' by Harper's comments
in House" CTV News.
https://www.ctvnews.ca/bains-baffled-by-harper-s-
comments-in-house-1.230837

N.n. (2008). "Nuclear safety watchdog head fired for
'lack of leadership': minister" CBC News.
https://www.cbc.ca/news/canada/nuclear-safety-
watchdog-head-fired-for-lack-of-leadership-
minister-1.748815

N.n. (2010). "Long-gun registry efficient: RCMP
report" CBC News.
https://www.cbc.ca/news/canada/long-gun-
registry-efficient-rcmp-report-1.886843

N.n. (2010). "Thousands protest Parliament's
suspension." CBC News.
https://www.cbc.ca/news/politics/thousands-
protest-parliament-s-suspension-1.866970

N.n. (2011). "A re-branding of the Harper
Government." CBC News.

https://www.cbc.ca/news/politics/a-rebranding-of-the-harper-government-1.1040716

N.n. (2011). "Harper government mislead Parliament on G8 spending: AG" Maclean's. http://www.macleans.ca/general/harper-government-misled-parliament-on-g8-spending-ag/

N.n. (2011). "Oda admits that she had a CIDA document altered." CBC. https://www.cbc.ca/news/canada/oda-admits-she-had-cida-document-altered-1.981211

N.n. (2011). Debunking Ignatieff's Iraq "Invasion Planning." https://afewtastefulsnaps.wordpress.com/2011/04/20/debunking-ignatieffs-iraq-invasion-planning/

N.n. (2012). "Online surveillance bill critics are siding with 'child pornographers': Vic Toews" National Post. http://news.nationalpost.com/news/canada/online-surveillance-bill-critics-are-siding-with-child-pornographers-vic-toews

N.n. (2012). "Veterans' Minister halted ombudsman privacy investigation" CBC News. https://www.cbc.ca/news/politics/veterans-minister-halted-ombudsman-s-privacy-investigation-1.1199025

N.n. (2012). Conservatives' 'in-and-out' scandal investigation cost taxpayers $2.3-million" National Post. http://news.nationalpost.com/news/canada/conserv

atives-in-and-out-scandal-investigation-cost-taxpayers-2-3m

N.n. (2012). Pickton Inquiry Slams 'Blatant Failures' by Police. Cbc News. retrieved from https://www.cbc.ca/news/canada/british-columbia/pickton-inquiry-slams-blatant-failures-by-police-1.1191108

N.n. (2013). "Government lawyer Edgar Schmidt courageously blows the whistle: Editorial." Toronto Star. https://www.thestar.com/opinion/editorials/2013/01/19/government_lawyer_edgar_schmidt_courageously_blows_the_whistle_editorial.html

N.n. (2013). "Harper government stonewalling spending analysis, budget officer says." National Post. https://nationalpost.com/news/politics/harper-government-stonewalling-spending-analysis-budget-officer-says

N.n. (2013). Those Who Take us Away: Abusive Policing and Failures in Protection of Indigenous Women and Girls in Northern British Columbia, Canada. Human Rights Watch. https://www.hrw.org/report/2013/02/13/those-who-take-us-away/abusive-policing-and-failures-protection-Indigenous-women

N.n. (2014). "Conservatives to change copyright law, allowing free use of news content in political ads" CTV News. https://www.ctvnews.ca/politics/conservatives-to-change-copyright-law-allowing-free-use-of-news-content-in-political-ads-1.2046197

N.n. (2014). "Fair Elections Act Protests Scheduled Across Canada Today" Huffington Post. http://www.huffingtonpost.ca/2014/04/26/fair-elections-act-protests_n_5219043.html

N.n. (2014). "New Bruce Carson charge linked to work at University of Calgary." CBC News. https://www.cbc.ca/news/canada/calgary/new-bruce-carson-charge-linked-to-work-at-university-of-calgary-1.2641759

N.n. (2014). "Charities under audit fire band together for answers from Canada Revenue Agency: Editorial" Toronto Star. https://www.thestar.com/opinion/editorials/2014/08/11/charities_under_audit_fire_band_together_for_answers_from_canada_revenue_agency_editorial.html

N.n. (2014). "Dean Del Mastro resigns his seat in House of Commons before vote to suspend him" National Post. http://news.nationalpost.com/news/canada/canadian-politics/dean-del-mastro-resigns-his-seat-in-house-of-commons-after-hes-found-guilty-of-violating-canada-elections-act

N.n. (2014). "Harper has picked a battle he can't win: former Harper aide." Global News. https://globalnews.ca/news/1323880/harpers-picked-a-battle-he-cant-win-former-harper-aide/

N.n. (2014). "Tories have spent millions in taxpayer funds on Facebook ads targeting Canadians" National Post. https://nationalpost.com/news/politics/tories-have-

spent-millions-in-taxpayer-funds-on-facebook-ads-
targeting-canadians

N.n. (2014). "Tory MP Brad Butt Admits Claim Of
Witnessing Voter Fraud Wasn't 'Accurate'."
Huffington Post.
https://www.huffingtonpost.ca/2014/02/24/brad-
butt-fair-elections-act-voter-
fraud_n_4848937.html?guccounter=1

N.n. (2014). Full Text of Peter Mansbridge's Interview
with Stephen Harper. CBC news.
https://www.cbc.ca/news/politics/full-text-of-peter-
mansbridge-s-interview-with-stephen-harper-
1.2876934

N.n. (2014). Harper Rebuffs Renewed Calls for
Murdered, Missing Women Inquiry. CBC News.
https://www.cbc.ca/news/canada/manitoba/harper-
rebuffs-renewed-calls-for-murdered-missing-
women-inquiry-1.2742845

N.n. (2015). "Latest Conservative ad could violate
government's own anti-terror law" CTV News.
https://www.ctvnews.ca/politics/latest-
conservative-ad-could-violate-government-s-own-
anti-terror-law-1.2440047

N.n. (2015). "Does Stephen Harper want to pick and
choose refugees based on their religion?"
PressProgress.
https://pressprogress.ca/does_stephen_harper_want
_to_pick_and_choose_refugees_based_on_their_re
ligion/

N.n. (2015). "Most Canadians opposed Conservative move to deny health care to refugees, internal poll shows". Press Progress. https://pressprogress.ca/most_canadians_opposed_conservative_move_to_deny_health_care_to_refugees_internal_poll_shows/

N.n. (2015). "National Post View: The PMO's selfish special forces blunder." National Post. https://nationalpost.com/opinion/national-post-view-the-pmos-selfish-special-forces-blunder

N.n. (2015). "National Post View: The PMO's selfish special forces blunder." National Post. https://nationalpost.com/opinion/national-post-view-the-pmos-selfish-special-forces-blunder

N.n. (2015). "Tribunal awards Cindy Blackstock $20,000 for suffering" MacLean's. http://www.macleans.ca/politics/ottawa/tribunal-rules-awards-cindy-blackstock-20000-for-suffering/

N.n. (2015). Aboriginal Statistics at a Glance. Retrieved from life-expectancy-esperance-vie-eng.htm

n.n. (2018). "The Arrival of the Europeans: 17th Century Wars," Government of Canada. Retrieved from https://www.canada.ca/en/department-national-defence/services/military-history/history-heritage/popular-books/aboriginal-people-canadian-military/arrival-europeans-17th-century-wars.html n.n. (2018). The Arrival of the Europeans: 17th Century Wars. Government of Canada. Retrieved from https://www.canada.ca/en/department-national-defence/services/military-history/history-heritage/popular-books/aboriginal-people-canadian-military/arrival-europeans-17th-century-wars.html

N.n. (2019), "Statement by the Prime Minister on terrorist attack on two mosques in New Zealand." *Justin Trudeau, Prime Minister of Canada.* https://pm.gc.ca/en/news/statements/2019/03/15/statement-prime-minister-terrorist-attack-two-mosques-new-zealand

n.n. (2020). Indian Act (Plain-Language Summary). In The Canadian Encyclopedia. https://thecanadianencyclopedia.ca/en/article/indian-act-plain-language-summary.

N.n. (2021). Canada's 2021 Nationally Determined Contribution Under the Paris Agreement. United Nations Framework Convention on Climate Change. Retrieved from Canada's Enhanced NDC Submission1_FINAL EN.pdf

N.n. (2021). Conservative Leader Erin O'Toole on Heartbreaking Discovery of Hundreds of Unmarked Graves in Saskatchewan. Conservative. https://www.conservative.ca/conservative-leader-erin-otoole-on-heartbreaking-discovery-of-hundreds-of-unmarked-graves-in-saskatchewan/

n.n. (2021). Conservative Statement on Liberal Carbon Tax Supreme Court Ruling. Conservative. Retrieved from

https://www.conservative.ca/conservative-statement-on-liberal-carbon-tax-supreme-court-ruling/

n.n. (n.d). "National Energy Program (1980-84)". *Alberta Tourism and Culture*. http://history.alberta.ca/energyheritage/gas/transformation/west-vs-east/nep.aspx

n.n. (n.d). Royal Mounted Police. *Government of Canada*. https://www.canada.ca/en/department-national-defence/corporate/reports-publications/proactive-disclosure/vac-estimates-budget/rcmp-estimates-budget.html

National Post. https://nationalpost.com/opinion/vanmala-subramaniam-before-you-declare-canada-is-not-a-racist-country-do-your-homework

Newport, F. (2019). "The Impact of Increased Political Polarization," Gallup. Retrieved from https://news.gallup.com/opinion/polling-matters/268982/impact-increased-political-polarization.aspx

Nicholson, Stephen P. (1 January 2012). "Polarizing Cues". American Journal of Political Science. 56 (1): 52–66. doi:10.1111/j.1540-5907.2011.00541.x

Nikiforuk, A. (2011). "Bruce Carson Scandal Greased by Harper's Oil Sands Agenda." The Tyee. https://thetyee.ca/News/2011/04/27/CarsonOilSands/

Nikiforuk, A. (2013). "Dismantling of Fishery Library 'Like a Book Burning,' Say Scientists." The Tyee.

https://thetyee.ca/News/2013/12/09/Dismantling-Fishery-Library/

Nikiforuk, A. (2013). "What's Driving Chaotic Dismantling of Canada's Science Libraries?" The Tyee. http://thetyee.ca/News/2013/12/23/Canadian-Science-Libraries/

Nikiforuk, A. (2013). "What's Driving Chaotic Dismantling of Canada's Science Libraries?" The Tyee. 2013. http://thetyee.ca/News/2013/12/23/Canadian-Science-Libraries/

Nikiforuk, A. (2014). "Scientists Say DFO's Library Closure Defence Doesn't Add Up." The Tyee. 2014. https://thetyee.ca/News/2014/01/08/Scientists-Say-DFOs-Library-Closure-Defence-Doesnt-Add-Up/

Noakes, T. (2006). National Energy Program. In *The Canadian Encyclopedia*. Retrieved from https://www.thecanadianencyclopedia.ca/en/article/national-energy-program

Noël, B. (2013). "Bloc Québécois". *The Canadian Encyclopedia.* https://www.thecanadianencyclopedia.ca/en/article/bloc-quebecois

O'Malley, K. (2015). "Taxpayer Group Urges Tories To Stop Pumping Public Money Into Partisan Ads" Huffington Post. https://www.huffingtonpost.ca/2015/03/18/taxpayer-group-urges-tori_n_6896326.html

O'Malley, K. (2015). Diane Finley Breached Conflict Rules, Federal Ethics Watchdog Rules. CBC News. Retrieved from https://www.cbc.ca/news/politics/diane-finley-breached-conflict-rules-federal-ethics-watchdog-rules-1.2988913

Paris, M. (2014). Chuck Strahl Steps Down as Spy Watchdog Amid Lobbying Questions. CBC News. https://www.cbc.ca/news/politics/chuck-strahl-steps-down-as-spy-watchdog-amid-lobbying-questions-1.2510321

Parole Board of Canada. (2008). The Canadian Multicultural Act. Government of Canada.

Parrott, Z.; Marshall, T. (2006). Iroquois Wars. The Canadian Encyclopedia. https://www.thecanadianencyclopedia.ca/en/article/iroquois-wars

Parry, T. (2014). SIRC Chair's Pipeline Lobbying Seen as Symptom of Larger Problem. CBC News. Retrieved from sirc-chair-s-pipeline-lobbying-seen-as-symptom-of-larger-problem-1.2489655

Partisanship and Political Animosity in 2016". Pew Research Center for the People and the Press. 2016-06-22. Retrieved May 14th, 2021

Patriquin, M. (2018). Canada: Holdout of Quebec Separatism Faces End of the Dream. The Guardian. https://www.theguardian.com/world/2018/sep/30/terrebonne-hold-out-of-quebec-separatism-faces-end-of-the-dream

Payton, L. (2011). Helena Guergis Broke Ethics Rules, Watchdog Says. CBC News. https://www.cbc.ca/news/politics/helena-guergis-broke-ethics-rules-watchdog-says-1.1055042

Payton, L. (2013). James Moore Sorry for Remarks about Hungry Children. CBC News. https://www.cbc.ca/news/politics/james-moore-sorry-for-remarks-about-hungry-children-1.2465666

Payton, L. (2013). Peter Penashue Quits Over Campaign Donations. CBC News. https://www.cbc.ca/news/politics/peter-penashue-quits-over-campaign-donations-1.1335297

Payton, L. (2014). "Bruce Carson, former PMO staffer, has banking records seized by RCMP." CBC News. https://www.cbc.ca/news/politics/bruce-carson-former-pmo-staffer-has-banking-records-seized-by-rcmp-1.2561271

Payton, L. (2015). Pamela Wallin's expense claims sought from 3 more organizations. CBC News. https://www.cbc.ca/news/politics/pamela-wallin-s-expense-claims-sought-from-3-more-organizations-1.3016760

Pedwell, T. (2013). "PMO backs down on plan to ban cameraman from trip" Toronto Star. https://www.thestar.com/news/canada/2013/10/02/pmo_appears_set_to_ban_tv_cameraman_from_trip_for_asking_question.html

Pedwell, T. (2014). "Interference by PMO emboldened Netflix against broadcast regulator,

experts say." CTV News.
https://winnipeg.ctvnews.ca/interference-by-pmo-emboldened-netflix-against-broadcast-regulator-experts-say-1.2019874

Peterson, D. (2013). MP Accused of Breaching Conflict Rules. Toronto.com.
https://www.toronto.com/news-story/3131562-mp-accused-of-breaching-conflict-rules

Phillips, O. (1982). "The Canada Act 1982," The International and Comparative Law Quarterly, 31(4), 845-848. Retrieved August 30, 2020, from http://www.jstor.org/stable/759411

Platt, Brian (June 5, 2018). "Ontario Proud, the right-wing Facebook giant in Ontario's election, eyes federal election involvement | National Post". National Post.

Postmedia News. (2013). "Federal librarians fear being 'muzzled' under new code of conduct that stresses 'duty of loyalty' to the government." National Post.
https://nationalpost.com/news/canada/library-and-archives-canada/

Postmedia News. (2013). "Letter warning Stephen Harper against appointing Arthur Porter to oversee spy agency raised no red flags." National Post.
https://nationalpost.com/news/politics/letter-warning-stephen-harper-against-appointing-arthur-porter-to-oversee-spy-agency-raised-no-red-flags

Powers, L. (2015). "Conservatives pledge funds, tip line to combat 'barbaric cultural practices'" CBC

News. https://www.cbc.ca/news/politics/canada-election-2015-barbaric-cultural-practices-law-1.3254118

Press Progress. (2015). Officer of Parliament warns Tory Bill Gives Government Power to Cover-Up Own Crimes. PressProgress. https://pressprogress.ca/watch_officer_of_parliament_warns_tory_bill_gives_government_power_to_cover_up_own_crimes/

Press Progress. (2015). : Conservative MP Uses "Air Quotes" to Dismiss C-51 Concerns from Legal Experts. Press Progress. https://pressprogress.ca/video_conservative_mp_uses_air_quotes_to_dismiss_c_51_concerns_from_legal_experts/

Press Progress. (2015). 6 Reasons Why You Need to Carefully Read the Small Print on Harper's Trans-Pacific Partnership Deal. Press Progress. https://pressprogress.ca/6_reasons_why_you_need_to_carefully_read_the_small_print_on_harpers_tpp_deal/

Press Progress. (2015). 6 Times Conservatives Insulted the Intelligence of Canadians Ramming Through Bill C-51. Press Progress. https://pressprogress.ca/6_times_conservatives_insulted_intelligence_canadians_ramming_through_c51/

Press Progress. (2015). Video Shows Conservative Campaign Team Tearing Down Election Signs. Press Progress. https://pressprogress.ca/does_this_video_show_a_c

onservative_campaign_team_tearing_down_electio
n_signs/

PressProgess. (2015). : Why Are Senators Allowed to
Raise Money for the Conservatives? Press
Progress.
https://pressprogress.ca/video_why_are_senators_a
llowed_to_raise_money_for_the_conservatives/

PressProgress. (2014). : Leona Aglukkaq's Bizarre
Response to News People Look For Food At
Garbage Dump. Press Progress.
https://pressprogress.ca/video_leona_aglukkaq_s_b
izarre_response_to_news_people_look_for_food_a
t_garbage_dump/

PressProgress. (2014). Peter MacKay Slapped Down
(Again) by Judge Over Victim Surcharge. Press
Progress.
https://pressprogress.ca/peter_mackay_slapped_do
wn_again_by_judge_over_victim_surcharge/

PressProgress. (2014). Was John Oliver's Job Creation
Plan that Creates No Jobs Outsourced to Business
Lobbyists. Press Progress.
https://pressprogress.ca/was_joe_oliver_s_job_crea
tion_plan_that_creates_no_jobs_outsourced_to_bu
siness_lobbyists/

PressProgress. (2015). Conservative Candidate
Repeatedly Photobombs Taxpayer-Funded Events.
Press Progress.
https://pressprogress.ca/conservative_candidate_re
peatedly_photobombs_taxpayer_funded_events/

PressProgress. (2015). Conservative MP Billed Taxpayers for Event Hosted by Same Anti-Tax Group He Used to Run. Press Progress. Retrieved from https://pressprogress.ca/conservative_mp_billed_ta xpayers_for_antitax_event_hosted_by_same_antita x_group_he_used_to_run/

PressProgress. (2015). Conservative Website Promotes Stephen Harper with Taxpayer-Funded '24/Seven' Videos. Press Progress. https://pressprogress.ca/conservative_website_pro motes_stephen_harper_with_taxpayer_funded_24_ seven_videos/

PressProgress. (2015). Deputy Speaker Admits Using Tax Dollars to Send Voters "Partisan" Conservative Mail. Press Progress. https://pressprogress.ca/deputy_speaker_admits_us ing_tax_dollars_to_send_voters_partisan_conserva tive_mail/

PressProgress. (2015). Did Taxpayers Cover Michelle Rempel's Trip to a Conservative Wine Tasting Fundraiser. Press Progress. https://pressprogress.ca/did_taxpayers_cover_mich elle_rempels_trip_to_a_conservative_wine_tasting _fundraiser/

PressProgress. (2015). Here are 86 Conservative Candidates who will Vote Against Women's Reproductive Rights. Press Progress. https://pressprogress.ca/here_are_86_conservative_ candidates_who_will_vote_against_womens_repro ductive_rights/

PressProgress. (2015). Job Minister Wears Partisan Polo Shirt to Official Government Announcement. Press Progress. https://pressprogress.ca/jobs_minister_wears_partis an_polo_shirt_to_official_government_announcem ent/

PressProgress. (2015). Pierre Poilevre Holds Taxpayer-Funded Photo-Op with Unelected Conservative Candidates. Press Progress. https://pressprogress.ca/pierre_poilievre_holds_tax payer_funded_photo_op_with_unelected_conserva tive_candidates/

PressProgress. (2015). VIDEO: Aboriginal Affairs Minister Literally Won't Stand Up for Missing and Murdered Women. Press Progress. https://pressprogress.ca/video_aboriginal_affairs_ minister_literally_won_t_stand_up_for_missing_a nd_murdered_women/

PressProgress. (2016). As Harper's CRA Audits Continue, Right-Wing Charities Report Zero 'Political Activity' Again. Press Progresshttps://pressprogress.ca/as_harper_cra_aud its_continue_right_wing_charities_report_zero_pol itical_activity_again/

PressProgress. (2016). James "Scrooge" Moore Talks Child Poverty. Press Progress. https://pressprogress.ca/james_scrooge_moore_talk s_child_poverty/

Proussalidis, D. (2013). Finance Minister Jim Flaherty Broke Conflict of Interest Rules: Ethics Watchdog.

Brantford Expositor.
https://www.brantfordexpositor.ca/2013/01/18/fina
nce-minister-jim-flaherty-broke-conflict-of-
interest-rules-ethics-watchdog

Pugliese, D. (2014). "Government orders federal
departments to keep tabs on all demonstrations
across the country" Ottawa Citizen.
https://ottawacitizen.com/news/politics/government
-orders-federal-departments-to-keep-tabs-on-all-
demonstrations-across-country

R. (2021). O'Toole Says Caucus will Both Respect and
Challenge House Vaccine Policy. CTV News.
https://www.ctvnews.ca/politics/o-toole-says-
caucus-will-both-respect-and-challenge-house-
vaccine-policy-1.5640593

Raj, A. (2013). "Trudeau Protest Was Manned By
Tory Interns And Organized By PMO" Huffington
Post.
http://www.huffingtonpost.ca/2013/06/25/trudeau-
protest-conservative-interns-pmo_n_3492852.html

Raj, A. (2019). Bernier Claims "Islamist Extremists"
Have Infiltrated Canadian Politics. Huffpost.
https://www.huffingtonpost.ca/entry/maxime-
bernier-
extremists_ca_5d5ad57de4b0d8840ff6bd77

Reicher, Stephen; Haslam, S. Alexander (November
19, 2016). "The politics of hope: Donald Trump as
an entrepreneur of identity". Scientific American.

Rennie, S. (2014). Senate Still Out $45,000 for Patrick
Brazeau's Expense Claims. The Globe and Mail.

https://www.theglobeandmail.com/news/politics/senate-still-out-45000-for-brazeaus-expense-claims/article21396455/

Reynolds. C. (2021). Raising Flags to Mark Residential Schools Legacy Commits Canada to be Better: O'Toole. CP24 News. raising-flags-to-mark-residential-schools-legacy-commits-canada-to-be-better-o-toole-1.5580707

Rezel, R. (2019). "Robocalls, ethics violations and other Scheer Scandals". *ThinkPol*. https://thinkpol.ca/2019/10/20/robocalls-ethics-violations-scheer-scandals/comment-page-1/

Rieger, S. (2019). "Maxime Bernier photographed with members of alleged hate group in Calgary". *CBC News*. https://www.cbc.ca/news/canada/calgary/maxime-bernier-northern-guard-1.5205881

Robinson, G. (2017). Internment of Japanese Canadians. The Canadian Encyclopedia. https://www.thecanadianencyclopedia.ca/en/article/internment-of-japanese-canadians

Rocher, F. (2014). "Self-determination and the Use of Referendums: The Case of Quebec," International Journal of Politics, Culture, and Society, 27(1), 25-45. August 29, 2020, http://www.jstor.org/stable/24713360

Rochester, J. (2003). Exploration in the Pacific North-West Before the American Presence. History. Retrieved from https://www.historylink.org/File/5449

Roman, K. (2010). "Tory logo on cheques goes too far: ethics chief" CBC News. https://www.cbc.ca/news/politics/tory-logo-on-cheques-goes-too-far-ethics-chief-1.951852

Rushkoff, D. (2010). Program or be programmed: Ten commands for a digital age. Berkeley, CA: Soft Skull Press.

Russell, F. (2014). "Absolute Power in the Hands of Just One Man." National Newswatch. https://www.nationalnewswatch.com/2014/11/12/absolute-power-in-the-hands-of-just-one-man/#.X1EiKXlKhdh

Russell, F. (2014). Absolute Power in the Hands of Just One Man. National Newswatch. Retrieved from https://www.nationalnewswatch.com/2014/11/12/absolute-power-in-the-hands-of-just-one-man/#.YLayFJNKire

Samphir, Harrison (July 23, 2019). "The Post Millennial joins Conservative party's online booster club". NOW Magazine.

Sandborn, T. (2015). "Harper's Conservatives No Friend to the Union Worker" The Tyee. https://thetyee.ca/Opinion/2015/07/17/Harper-No-Friend-to-Union-Workers/

Sartori, Giovanni (1966). "European political parties: the case of polarized pluralism". Political Parties and Political Development: 137–176

Sartori, Giovanni (1976). Parties and party systems: a framework for analysis([Nouvelle édition] ed.). Colchester: ECPR.

Scheel E. V. (2020). "More Controversial Articles Surface from Kenney Speechwriter Accused of Racist, Sexist, and Homophobic Remarks," CBC news. Retrieved from https://www.cbc.ca/news/canada/calgary/kenney-speechwriter-bunner-controversial-comments-trend-1.5633079

Scott, M. (2014). "Quebec's Battle Against Conscription was a Defining Moment, Sowing the Seeds of Resentment that 50 Years Later Would Sprout into the Independence Movement," The Great War. Retrieved from http://ww1.canada.com/home-front/quebecs-conscription-crisis-divided-french-and-english-canada

Siddiqui, H. (2015). "Stephen Harper plays the politics of hate against Muslims" Toronto Star. https://www.thestar.com/opinion/commentary/2015/02/14/stephen-harper-plays-the-politics-of-hate-against-muslims.html?li_source=LI&li_medium=star_web_ymbii

Siddiqui, H. (2016). "How Harper systematically mined anti-Muslim prejudices". Toronto Star. https://www.thestar.com/news/insight/2016/04/10/how-harper-systematically-mined-anti-muslim-prejudices.html

Simpson, J. (2013). "Our money for attack ads – how low can the Harper Conservatives go?" The Globe and Mail. https://www.theglobeandmail.com/opinion/our-money-for-attack-ads-how-low-can-the-harper-conservatives-go/article11579462/

Sisk, Timothy D. (January 1989). "White politics in South Africa: politics under pressure". Africa Today. Indiana University Press. 36 (1): 29–39.

Smith, D. (2013). "War Measures Act," *The Canadian Encyclopedia*. https://www.thecanadianencyclopedia.ca/en/article/war-measures-act

Solomon, E.; Everson, k. (2014). 7 Environmental Charities Face Canada Revenue Agency Audits. CBC News. Retrieved from https://www.cbc.ca/news/politics/7-environmental-charities-face-canada-revenue-agency-audits-1.2526330

Somer, Murat; McCoy, Jennifer (2019). "Transformations through Polarizations and Global Threats to Democracy". The Annals of the American Academy of Political and Social Science. 681 (1): 8–22.

Stacey, C. (2013). Second World War (WWII). In The Canadian Encyclopedia. https://www.thecanadianencyclopedia.ca/en/article/second-world-war-wwii

Star Editorial Board. (2021). What a Mess Erin O'Toole has Made on Carbon Pricing. Toronto

Star.
https://www.thestar.com/opinion/editorials/2021/0
4/19/what-a-mess-erin-otoole-has-made-on-
carbon-pricing.html

Stevens, Geoffrey. (2014). "Senate scandal is far from
over." The Record.
https://www.therecord.com/opinion/columnists/201
4/03/10/senate-scandal-is-far-from-over.html

Strong-Boag, V. (2016). "Women's Suffrage in
Canada," The Canadian Encyclopedia.
https://www.thecanadianencyclopedia.ca/en/article/
suffrage

Struthers, J (2013). The Great Depression in Canada.
The Canadian Encyclopedia.
https://www.thecanadianencyclopedia.ca/en/article/
great-depression

Subramaniam, V. (2020). "Vanmala Subramaniam:
Before you declare Canada is not a racist country,
do your homework".

Tam Cho, Wendy K.; Gimpel, James G. (1 April
2007). "Prospecting for (Campaign) Gold" (PDF).
American Journal of Political Science. 51 (2): 255–
268.

Tardi, C. (2019). The Kyoto Protocol. Investopedia.
https://www.investopedia.com/terms/k/kyoto.asp

Tasker, J. P. (2021). Parliament Returns Today with a
Familiar Seat Map but a New Set of Challenges.
CBC News.
https://www.cbc.ca/news/politics/parliament-
returns-today-new-challenges-1.6255878

Tasker, J. P. & Poisson, J. (2021). Erin O'Toole says Conservatives' Rejection of Climate Change Resolution was 'a Distraction.' CBC News. Retrieved from otoole-climate-change-resolution-1.6031239

Tasker, J. P. (2020). "Senator calls on RCMP commissioner to resign after comments on systemic racism". CBC News. https://www.cbc.ca/news/politics/senator-rcmp-commissioner-resign-1.5612939

Tasker, J. P. (2020). "Systemic racism exists in the RCMP, Commissioner Brenda Lucki says". CBC News. https://www.cbc.ca/news/politics/brenda-lucki-systemic-racism-rcmp-1.5610355

Tassinari. P. (1995). Broken Promises- The High Artic Location. The NFB. https://www.nfb.ca/film/broken_promises_-_the_high_arctic_relocation/

Taylor, S. (2021). Erin O'Toole Says COVID-19 Vaccine Comments by Tory MPs Gladu, Lewis are not Helpful. CP24. erin-o-toole-says-covid-19-vaccine-comments-by-tory-mps-gladu-lewis-are-not-helpful-1.5657088

The Canadian Press. (2010). "Tories block staff from testifying at Parliamentary committees." Toronto Star. https://www.thestar.com/news/canada/2010/05/25/tories_block_staff_from_testifying_at_parliamentary_committees.html

The Canadian Press. (2012). "Federal bureaucrats pose as new citizens on Sun News." CBC News. https://www.cbc.ca/news/politics/federal-bureaucrats-pose-as-new-citizens-on-sun-news-1.1271079

The Canadian Press. (2013). Former Conservative MP Jay Hill Broke Conflict of Interest Rules: Ethics Watchdog. CTV News. Retrieved from https://www.ctvnews.ca/canada/former-conservative-mp-jay-hill-broke-conflict-of-interest-rules-ethics-watchdog-1.1212510

The Canadian Press. (2014). "Tory MP Maurice Vellacott Rebels Against Government 'Muzzling'." Huffington Post. https://www.huffingtonpost.ca/2014/01/27/maurice-vellacott-harper-muzzling_n_4676307.htm

The Canadian Press. (2014). Tory Senator Violated Conflict of Interest Code when he Helped Former Girlfriend get Sick Leave: Ethics Office. National Post. https://nationalpost.com/news/politics/tory-senator-violated-conflict-of-interest-code-when-he-helped-former-girlfriend-get-sick-leave-ethics-office

The Canadian Press. (2015). Companies Admit Illegal Contributions to Peter Penashue Campaign. CBC News. https://www.cbc.ca/news/politics/companies-admit-illegal-contributions-to-peter-penashue-campaign-1.3158576

The Canadian Press. (2015). Conservative MP Rick Dysktra Denies Claim He Bought Alcohol for

Underage Girls at Nightclub. National Post. Retrieved from https://nationalpost.com/news/politics/conservative -mp-rick-dykstra-denies-claim-he-bought-alcohol-for-underage-girls-at-nightclub

The Canadian Press. (2017). "TransCanada Cancels $15.7B Energy East Pipelines Project," Calgary Herald. https://calgaryherald.com/business/energy/transcan ada-cancels-energy-east-pipeline-

The Canadian Press. (2020). Man Accused in Rideau Hall Crash Had Rifle, Shotguns, and Threatened PM: RCMP. Canada's National Observer. man-accused-rideau-hall-crash-had-rifle-shotguns-and-threatened-pm-rcmp

The Canadian Press. (n.d.) "'Principled' Tory staffer refused to help Nigel Wright, PMO secretly tinker with Senate report on Mike Duffy." National Post. http://news.nationalpost.com/news/canada/canadia n-politics/principled-tory-staffer-refused-to-help-nigel-wright-pmo-secretly-tinker-with-senate-report-on-mike-duffy

The editors of Encyclopedia Britannica. (2020). Humphrey Gilbert. Britannica. https://www.britannica.com/biography/Humphrey-Gilbert.

The Editors of Encyclopedia Britannica. (2021). Kim Campbell. Encyclopedia Britannica. https://www.britannica.com/biography/Kim-Campbell

The Hamilton Spectator. (2018). The Long and Forgotten History of Muslims in Canada. The Hamilton Spectator. https://www.thespec.com/news/hamilton-region/2018/10/08/the-long-and-forgotten-history-of-muslims-in-canada.html

Tomlinson, A. (2020). "Raising a young Black man in North America today means fear, faith and hope that change will come". CBC News. https://www.cbc.ca/news/canada/raising-young-black-man-1.5594179

Tritton, A. (2013). The Great Migration of Canada. Exodus. https://www.exodus2013.co.uk/the-great-migration-of-canada/

Troper, H. (2017). Immigration in Canada. *The Canadian Encyclopedia.* https://www.thecanadianencyclopedia.ca/en/article/immigration

Tunney, C. & Zimonjic, P. (2019). "Trudeau pushes back on SNC-Lavalin, says he was 'surprised and disappointed' by Wilson-Raybould's resignation," CBC News. https://www.cbc.ca/news/politics/wilson-rayboul-snc-lavalin-1.5015755

Tunney, C. (2020). "Systemic racism exists in RCMP, Trudeau argues — after commissioner says she's 'struggling' with the term". CBC News. https://www.cbc.ca/news/politics/rcmp-systemic-racism-lucki-trudeau-1.5607622

Turnbull, S. (2021). Conservative MP's Comments about Vaccination, COVID-19 spread 'not appropriate': O'Toole. CTV News. conservative-mp-s-comments-about-vaccination-covid-19-spread-not-appropriate-o-toole-1.5656790

Ura, Joseph Daniel; Ellis, Christopher R. (10 February 2012). "Partisan Moods: Polarization and the Dynamics of Mass Party Preferences". The Journal of Politics. 74(1): 277–291.

Valiante, G. (2019). "SNC-Lavalin," The Canadian Encyclopedia. https://www.thecanadianencyclopedia.ca/en/article/snc-lavalin

Verrette, M. (2006). Manitoba Schools Question. In The Canadian Encyclopedia. https://www.thecanadianencyclopedia.ca/en/article/manitoba-schools-question

Verrette, M. (2006). Manitoba Schools Question. The Canadian Encyclopedia. https://www.thecanadianencyclopedia.ca/en/article/manitoba-schools-question

Villani, M. (2020). Calgary's South Asian Community Demands Premier Apology After 'Wake up Call' Comments. CTV News. Calgary-s-south-asian-community-demands-premier-apologize-after-wake-up-call-comments-1.5210563

Vomiero, J. (2019). "Scheer criticized after New Zealand mosque attack statement neglects to mention the word 'Muslim'" Global News.

https://globalnews.ca/news/5063385/scheer-statement-new-zealand-attack-muslim/

Waite, P. (2006). Pacific Scandal. In The Canadian Encyclopedia. https://www.thecanadianencyclopedia.ca/en/article/pacific-scandal

Waite, P. (2013). Confederation. In The Canadian Encyclopedia. https://www.thecanadianencyclopedia.ca/en/article/confederation.

Warnica, R. (2015). "The life and bloody death of Andrew Loku: Toronto police officer's face 'went white as a ghost' after shooting". National Post. https://nationalpost.com/news/toronto/the-life-and-bloody-death-of-andrew-loku

Warren, M. (2015). "Prepare to suffer the attacks." Toronto Sun. https://torontosun.com/2015/03/08/prepare-to-suffer-the-attacks.

Watters, H. (2015). "C-51, controversial anti-terrorism bill, is now law. So, what changes?" CBC News. https://www.cbc.ca/news/politics/c-51-controversial-anti-terrorism-bill-is-now-law-so-what-changes-1.3108608

Wells, P. (2013). "Why Conservatives think the public service is Liberal" MacLean's. http://www.macleans.ca/politics/ottawa/why-conservatives-think-the-public-service-is-liberal/

Wherry, A. (2014).. Interview: Brent Rathgeber on our irresponsible governance. Maclean's.

https://www.macleans.ca/politics/the-rathgeber-
reckoning/

Wherry, A. (2015). "Why the Tories said no to a star
candidate in Newfoundland," MacLeans's.
http://www.macleans.ca/news/canada/why-the-
tories-said-no-to-a-star-candidate-in-
newfoundland/

Whitaker, R. (2013) Pierre Elliott Trudeau. In The
Canadian Encyclopedia. Retrieved from
https://www.thecanadianencyclopedia.ca/en/article/
pierre-elliott-trudeau

Whittington, L. & Brennan, R. J. (2010). Brian
Mulroney Acted Inappropriately in Accepting Cash
Inquiry Finds. The Star.
https://www.thestar.com/news/canada/2010/05/31/
brian_mulroney_acted_inappropriately_in_accepti
ng_cash_inquiry_finds.html

Woods, Mel (June 11, 2020). "Erin O'Toole's 'Take
Back Canada' Slogan Prompts Plenty Of
Questions". HuffPost.

Woolf, M. (2021). Tories to Oppose Hybrid Parliament
Proposal, Say it Weakens Government Scrutiny.
Global News. Retrieved from
https://globalnews.ca/news/8397965/tories-oppose-
hybrid-parliament-proposal/

Wright, T. (2020). "First Nations Coalition Speaks Out
Against Call to Lift Sen. Lynn Beyak's
Suspension," Global News.
https://globalnews.ca/news/7133191/senator-lynn-
beyak-suspension-lift/

Yuan, Elaine Jingyan (2007). The New Multi-channel Media Environment in China: Diversity of Exposure in Television Viewing. Northwestern University.

Zhou, S. (2015). "Bill C-24 and the politics of citizenship," CBC News. https://www.cbc.ca/news/canada/manitoba/bill-c-24-and-the-politics-of-citizenship-1.3260618

Zimonjic, P. & Cullen, C. (2020). Erin O'Toole Walks Back Claim that Residential Schools were Designed to 'Provide Education." CBC News. Retrieved from erin-otoole-residential-schools-comments-1.5844307

Index